Evangelism

By
G Campbell Morgan

Dedication

To the faculties and students of Hartford, Chicago, Berkeley and Dayton theological seminaries 1903-1904.

To whom it was my pleasure and privilege to speak on Evangelism at their request, these stenographic reports of those ad dresses are dedicated with the earnest hope that they may be of some service in at least one branch of the ministry of the future.

G Campbell Morgan

Parvus Magna Press

5 Ambleside Close, Leyton, London, E10 5RU
Email: sic@pmpress.co.uk
Website: www.pmpress.co.uk

G Campbell Morgan wrote this book many years ago and it is now public domain. However, a lot of work went into the digitizing of the text – so whilst we don't mind if you re-use it – please ask if you wish to reprint!

If you like this edition and you have an idea of another you would like to see please let us know!!

British Library Cataloguing in Publication Data

A catalogue record and a copy of this book are available from the British Library

ISBN: 978-1-910372-16-6 Paperback

Parvus Magna Press publishes limited run and niche interest books in the UK. If you would like to see your book in print, please email your manuscript to sic@pmpress.co.uk

The Master's Men

All the books in The Master's Men series are now public domain, they are the classics of a bygone era when the very foundations of the Evangelical faith were being laid down.

D L Moody, Finney, Billy Sunday range alongside great thinkers like G Campbell Morgan and Philipps Brooks (a personal favourite).

When these men preached, and when they wrote, it was obvious to all who they served – they were The Masters Men!

We have also included in the series some older more Catholic books where the salvation and service of the author is obvious to all who read them

We edited these books in very minor way – just changing the Roman numbering system and if necessary a light touch on the text to aid a better understanding of the authors aim.

We hope you enjoy this series and if you can think of anything else you would like to see – let us know!

Sharif George
Editor

Free eBook

As part of our commitment to helping you get the most from your Evangelical Heritage Library purchase we are happy to supply a free electronic copy of this book by email or for download from our website.

To claim your free copy of the electronic version of this book, please email sales@pmpress.co.uk with the title of the book you have purchased and where you bought it from and we will send it straight to you.

About G Campbell Morgan

Doctor George Campbell Morgan D.D. lived from 1863 – 1945); he was a British evangelist, preacher and a leading Bible scholar.

Morgan apparently preached his first sermon when he was 13 as a direct result of hearing Evangelist D L Moody in London.

Morgan was the pastor of Westminster Chapel in London from 1904 to 1919, and from 1933 to 1943.

A prolific scholar and author, Morgan penned dozens of books that distributed widely here in the UK and in the US.

Dr Morgan's easy style and evangelical approach to the word of God and to the church ministry is as refreshing and relevant today as it was in the 1900's.

You can even detect some of D L Moody's influence in these pages...

Contents

About G Campbell Morgan 7
Evangelism 9
    The Old Evangel 9
    The New Evangel 10
The Church Evangelistic 25
The Evangelist. 39
The Evangelistic Service. 57
The Present Opportunity. 77
Also by Parvus Magna Press 89
The Evangelical Heritage Library 90

Evangelism

The Old Evangel

The hour is characterized by renewed interest in evangelistic work. Men of all shades of opinion, and men who do not seem to have very profound opinions of any sort, are nevertheless turning their attention towards the great subject of evangelism. I suppose there are a few people in the Christian Church who have no particular interest in the subject. All I can say of such is, that they are living in the mental mood of at least ten years ago.

A new interest in evangelistic work is manifesting itself in different ways. Some people are giving themselves to prayer, that God will give us "an old-fashioned revival." On the other hand, a great many people, equally devoted and sincere, yet who are out of harmony with what they speak of as the older methods of theological thinking, are nevertheless looking for some visitation. These, instead of praying for an old-fashioned revival are attempting to forecast the lines of what they call "the new evangelism."

Now I do not want to be unkindly critical, for I am profoundly conscious that the underlying fact in each case is of supreme value, but I would never pray for an old-fashioned revival, nor would I attempt to forecast the lines of a new evangelism. But why not pray for an old-fashioned revival? Because I want God's next new thing. Then why not forecast the lines of a new evangelism? Because one evangel is enough for all time.

If a man is praying for an old-fashioned revival, in all probability when God's visitation comes, he will not be conscious of it. I can quite imagine how forty years ago, men remembering the marvellous movement under

Finney, might have prayed for an old-fashioned revival such as that which accompanied his preaching.

Then it is more than likely that when God raised up Dwight Lyman Moody, such men would be out of sympathy with all his methods for a long while, for the notes of the two movements were utterly different. Or to go back still further before the great awakening under Finney, perhaps some prayed for an old-fashioned revival, like that under Wesley and Whitefield. If so, they almost certainly lacked sympathy with the new notes at first.

God fulfils Himself in many ways. In every new awakening there are fresh manifestations of God, a new unfolding of truth meeting the requirements of the age. The evangel is always fresh as the break of day, and yet as old as the continuity of day-break through the ages. We ought to be so living that when God begins His great triumphant march, we shall fall in with the first battalion, and have part in the first victories.

The New Evangel

It is equally false to speak of a new evangelism, because there is to be no new evangel. When I read what that very brilliant, and very devoted Christian man, Dr. John Watson, says the lines of the new evangelism are to be, I am in agreement with all he does say, and out of agreement in that there are things he does not say. All he says is true. But there are important things he omits. The next great movement will have within it the notes of the social and the ethical. But there will not be omitted from it the notes of blood redemption, and spiritual regeneration. These are the truths we have to keep in mind.

When I hear of men speaking of a new evangelism, it is well to ask their definition of the term evangelism. When I see that Mr. B. Fay Mills has gone out into evangelistic work the first impulse of the heart is to rejoice. But when I find that he is simply preaching a doctrine of a social kingdom, without insistence upon the necessity for regeneration, then it is time we declare our separation.

To say that the new evangelism is to be ethical, and by that to seem to criticise the old, is to prove a misunderstanding of the old, and also a misunderstanding of the deepest necessity of the times in which we live and serve. When a man tells me, the next revival will be ethical, does he mean to say that the last was not? If the great movements under Wesley, Whitefield, Finney, Moody were not ethical, what were they? They were movements that took hold of vast masses of men, and moved them out of back streets into front ones, and if that was not ethical, surely nothing can be so. Beginning with the regeneration of the man, they changed his environment, and made him a citizen of whom any city might have been proud. That is the true ethical note.

In approaching a constructive statement concerning the evangel, I must ask you to take two things for granted: first, the finality of Christianity; and secondly, that the New Testament is the authoritative interpretation thereof.

By the finality of Christianity, I mean that the writer of the letter to the Hebrews is correct in his estimate as declared in his opening sentences. God speaks to man. He has spoken to men in the past in divers portions, and in divers manners. All the messages of prophets, seers, and psalmists, of rites, ceremonies, and symbols were but broken lights of essential truth. But He has spoken unto us by His Son, and He has no more to say to men than He has said in Jesus Christ.

That does not mean for a single moment that we have perfectly understood the message of the Son yet. I believe that there is more light and truth to break out from the words of Jesus, and from the fact of Christ in the world, than men have ever seen. But God has said everything He has to say, and any new so-called revelation in conflict with that spoken by God in His Son is thereby proven to be not of the Spirit of God, but from beneath and of the devil.

In the second place it must also be accepted that the New Testament is the authoritative interpretation of Christianity. I hear a good deal today about the Christian consciousness as the true court of appeal in matters of faith and practice. I am searching for that Christian consciousness. Is it that of the Pope, or my own? Is it consensus of opinion? Then where shall I find it ex pressed? I decline to accept it as expressed in any creed. Where then is it?

The fact is that the Christian consciousness is a variable quantity according to differing experiences, and is I therefore wholly unreliable as a criterion of creed or character or conduct.

The Christian consciousness must ever be judged by a standard, and that is to be found in the New Testament. If you once take away the New Testament as the final court of appeal in matters of faith and practice, you will lose the Christian consciousness in half a century. It has been done once. The New Testament was lost to the churches in the dark ages. Then Luther arose, and following the restoration of the New Testament there came back the Christian consciousness. The court of appeal is the New Testament.

What is the Christian evangel? There is a preliminary question which I shall first attempt to answer. What is an evangel? This word evangel has come to us from the Latin *evangelium*, which simply means a gospel, for the word was introduced to the language during the ecclesiastical period.

So we must pass back behind this word as it came to us from the Latin, and find it as it stands upon the pages of our Greek Testament. There it simply means a good message. A good message! There is no note of sadness in an evangel. There is not a tone of terror in an evangel. An evangel is good news. An evangel is a good message.

In the New Testament the thought is invariably that of glad tidings, of good news, of a message that ought to fill the hearts of those who hear it with hope and gladness and joy.

The word, and cognate words, are used by the writers of the New Testament who deal specially with the subject of the work of Christ in its first application to the needs of men. And these words are singularly absent from those writings which deal with the deeper truths of Christian experience.

Take the Gospels, which we speak of as synoptic, Matthew, Mark, and Luke, and you will find the words recurring all the way through, evangel, or evangelist, or some cognate word.

But in the Gospel of John, the word is never used simply because the Gospel of John deals with the mystery of Christ's Person, and this can only be appreciated by those born again.

The evangel is the wicket gate of the kingdom. So also with the other writings. Paul, and Peter in his first epistle, and the writer of the letter to the Hebrews have these words, and this because they are in all these writings dealing with the initial facts.

But they are signally absent from the writings of John and James and Jude, and the second letter of Peter. All this indicates the principal thought of evangelism, and the value of the word as it lies in the New Testament.

The evangel is not denunciatory of sin. It is not pronunciatory of punishment. It is annunciatory of salvation. That is its great value.

This is not to say that the preacher will not have to discuss the subject of sin, will not have to proclaim the punishment of sin. But it is to say that the preacher who deals with and denounces sin, will never end his message with such denunciation. He proclaims God's evangel when he announces the fact that Christ is able to save from sin, and consequently from its penalty.

So also the evangelist may have, and indeed will have to deal with the severer aspects of truth. He will have to tell men that to those who have heard the evangel, to those who have been confronted with the claims of Jesus Christ, there can be no escape if they turn their back upon that which is God's uttermost in the way of saving men. But he will never proclaim that alone. He must super-add the great and glorious and hopeful declaration that their sins were borne by the One Who hung on the tree, and being so borne, in the infinite mercy and justice of God they may go free.

An evangel, therefore, is good news to such as need it. Joy is in it, the note of hope, of optimism. It comes to a man in the darkness, and brings him light. It comes to a man in bondage, and announces the way of escape. It comes to a man under the sentence of death, and tells him that the sentence has been remitted.

What then is the Christian evangel as revealed to us in the New Testament? It has four essential notes.

The first is that of a vision; the second, that of a value; the third, that of a virtue; and the fourth, that of a victory. The evangel proclaims first, the Lordship of Christ; secondly, the Cross of Christ; thirdly, the resurrection of Christ; and finally an indwelling Christ by the Holy Spirit.

First, the Lordship of Jesus.

Now you may say to me, but have you put these in their right order? Is it not true that the first business of the evangel is to preach the Cross of Christ? I do not think so.

I believe that the first note of the true evangel is that of announcing to men the Lordship of Christ. I am quite willing to grant you that very largely that has been omitted from much evangelistic preaching which has been blessed by God, and yet I am profoundly convinced that the evangelist who is going to take hold of the masses must return to the old apostolic method of preaching Jesus as Lord first.

But it may be objected He cannot be Lord of a man's life until the man is saved. Quite true, but the vast majority of people will never begin to feel their need of His salvation until they have been brought to stand in the light of the claim of His Lordship, and so I insist upon the putting of this first.

This was the apostolic method. In the second chapter of the Acts of the Apostles we have the first sermon preached in the power of the outpoured Spirit, which is a perfect pattern for true Christian homiletics to the end of time.

It is from first to last an appeal to the men who were listening. Peter was not preaching in front of the people and wondering whether they would like it. He was preaching to them. And the difference between the preaching that does nothing and the preaching that does something is the difference between preaching before people, and preaching to people.

Let us look at its structure. It has two divisions. First, "This is that." Secondly, "He hath shed forth this."

"This is that which was spoken by the prophet Joel," the present manifestation set in its relation to old time prophesying. This day of Pentecost is the fulfilment of the past.

"He hath shed forth this." The past was fulfilled through Jesus. He was the centre, and heart, and life of the first sermon.

And the final word of the sermon, to which everything led up was, "Let all the house of Israel therefore know assuredly, that God hath made Him both Lord and Christ, this Jesus Whom ye crucified."

Thus on the day of Pentecost Peter was proclaiming the Lordship of Christ. Confronting blind belief, and flippant scepticism, and idle curiosity, and surging sorrow, and blinding sin, and masterful passion, and everything else, he said "Jesus is Lord." That was the first note.

The evangelist, therefore, has first to confront this age and say to it, There is one King, one Lord, one Master, one seat of authority, one tribunal to which men may make their appeal. One Who upholds in His hands the balance of justice, from Whose verdict there can be no appeal, and Who is at this moment the Lord Jesus Christ.

This is not a small theme. Start to preach that, and you will find you will not finish it next Sunday morning; no, nor in a month's sermons. Buddha and Confucius will have a great rest, and Browning and Tennyson and all the others with their rush lights will not allure you from the great essential light, the Lordship of Jesus Christ.

We have not merely to claim that Jesus is Lord, but we have to demonstrate that He is Lord. We have to show to this age in the light of a new century, with all its advance, and progress, and civilization, that Jesus Christ is Lord not merely because God has appointed Him King —though that is true—but because of His inherent royalty. God did not appoint Jesus to Kingship capriciously. He appointed Him to Kingship because He is King in the very fibre of His nature, in the very fact of His personality.

We challenge the world today, and we say that the Jesus of the New Testament, the Jesus of the virgin birth, the virtuous life, the vicarious dying, and the victorious resurrection, stands amid this age, with all its fierce light, its boasted civilization, and its new psychology, facile princeps, the crowned Lord because of the supernal glory of His own character.

But you tell me that these things are not authentic, that you have abandoned the Gospel of John, that Matthew and Mark and Luke are not to be trusted, and that in all probability that Man never existed. Very well. Then my business is to find the man who imagined this Man, for the man who imagined Him must be as great as the Man imagined.

You do not get away from the Person revealed when you think you have done away with the books. He stands out in the midst of this age, our Master and Lord, and there never has been one like Him. And you and I have to tell men to test all sides of their nature by Jesus Christ.

They have to bring up to His royalty their intellect, their emotion, their will. They have to test their creed, their character, their conduct by Him. He has moved into this new century with all its electric gaudiness, with the supernal loveliness of the King of men. And no man dare come into the presence of the Man of Nazareth revealed in the Gospels, and say, I am mightier or better than Thou, or, I know more than Thou knowest, O Man of Nazareth. He is the Lord of men, and our business is to proclaim it, to insist upon it, to die for it if need be.

But if you stop there you are not preaching the Gospel. See what follows. If Jesus is indeed preached as Lord, there must always be as the issue of it an application of the truth to individual needs. No man ever yet stood searched by the light of that revelation of life without having to bow his head with shame, and say, I am a sinner. To preach the living Lordship of Christ is to create the necessity for His Cross. Do we sufficiently realize this?

If I said that the first note of the evangel is the Lord ship of Christ, I am quite willing to grant that the heart of the evangel is the Cross. This age is peculiarly characterized by a loose sense of sin amongst men.

Today we have to preach to people who are not really willing to admit that they are sinners: pleasant, refined, cultured people, whom we hardly feel inclined to tell that they are sinners, and who, if we did, would not feel quite like believing it. There are people who will never have any I consciousness of sin as long as we keep them at Mount Sinai.

But there is not a man but that, if you bring him into the presence of Jesus Christ, and say That is your King, His law is your standard, His realization of life is your ideal, will go down in the presence of that and will say, I am a sinner.

I have the profoundest sympathy for the young man in the Gospel who said, "All these things have I kept from my youth up." I was born in a Christian family, and through that gracious fact—never to be undervalued—was strangely and wonderfully delivered from many of the more vulgar methods of sin, and I want to say to you, in all honesty, and all sincerity, I never trembled when I heard the law of Moses. But when I came into the presence of the radiant loveliness of Christ, when I heard his teaching, when I saw His perfection, then I said, If that is what I ought to be, O my God, how have I sinned! I stand in the presence of an external ethical code such as that of Moses, and I do not tremble. But whenever I come near the Incarnate Purity, into the presence of the Incarnate Love, I am ashamed, debased, bowed in the dust.

Brethren, we must preach Christ as Lord, and there will come to our people a sense of sin, a consciousness of inability, of failure, of break down. There is no other way of bringing men into this consciousness.

Then, thank God, we have the next note of the evangel. Oh, how shall we tell it? May God keep us living so near to it that it shall always be to us an element of astonishment!

> " Were the whole realm of Nature mine,
> That were a present far too small,
> Love so amazing, so Divine,
> Demands my life, my soul, my all."

"Love so amazing!" Are we amazed at that Love? Are we astonished at that Love? Think of it, that ideally perfect One, that infinite Lord and Master, went down to death. If you are only preaching His Lordship, that is not enough. If all you have to preach to men is His example, that is not enough.

Unless there is all that the New Testament claims there is in that death, then that death is the severest reflection upon the goodness of God that the world has ever seen. Unless there is a meaning in it, such as the New Testament declares to be in it, then in the presence of the Cross, I lose my faith in God. If death is simply the tragic ending of so beautiful a life, and nothing more, then God has done nothing when He ought to have done something.

But when I take the New Testament, and see what Christ says about His own death, and what the inspired writers of the New Testament say, and when there comes superadded to the Christ's estimate and the estimate of the apostles, the answer of my heart to the inner meaning of the Cross, then I know that the Cross is the heart and centre of a great evangel.

We are to tell men we fail, but the One Who never failed took our place. You cannot get away from the words vicarious atonement. The Cross is supremely the heart and centre of our great evangel.

But I am told today that there are men so cultured and refined that they do not care to talk about blood; men who cut out from the singing of the Church such hymns as, "There is a fountain filled with blood," who object to sing, "Not all the blood of beasts."

Why do you object to those things? You say they lack refinement? Refinement! Do you go to the Cross for refinement? You go to the Cross to see what sin is. Is blood objectionable? Of course it is. Is the brutal murder of a perfect man awful? Certainly it is. But why was it necessary? Because of sin.

Sin is not refined, and I come to the Cross to know the meaning of my own sin. I find my sin when I stand in the presence of the light of the Cross. But I never know its meaning until I see the Lord Christ crucified. Certainly there is no refinement in it. We must get back to the Cross to know all its ruggedness, to know all its brutality, its blood-baptism. It is only there that the heart finds the conscience cleaned.

I am going to put this superlatively. I am talking out of my deepest conviction when I say that if God would forgive me without the Cross then I never can be satisfied with His forgiveness. My own conscience is not at rest. There is that sin in the past, and if God says, I will forgive on the basis of pity, that is not enough, for it is there still.

But when God says to me, it is not there, He, the Son of My love took it. He in Whom was no sin, was made sin, and in the passion of His death, in the agony of His baptism, in the blood of the brutal Cross, all of which had no place in His life, He was dealing with your sin, then my heart begins its song, the song that will never end while eternity lasts. My conscience demands this Cross, and God answers that deepest human consciousness of mine, which He Himself had made. We must be very suspicious of any new evangel that has no Cross in it.

There is yet another thing, and I am trying to trace them as they come in the order of experience. A man stands erect until he sees the vision of the Lord Jesus Christ, and then he is afraid until he sees the value of the Cross of Christ, and he says, I am a sinner forgiven.

Now what else? I have to live in the same place, in the midst of circumstances against me, suffering the same temptations, still within the midst of forces which will entice me to sin, though I am forgiven.

Then we must preach the value of the resurrection, that He "brought life and immortality to light," that men may have life, not merely eternal life, but life as a force and virtue, a power and possibility in the life.

I like my Lord's words better than any other, "I came that they may have life, and may have it abundantly ... I lay down My life for the sheep and if I lay it down, I will take it again." And that is what He did, He laid it down in death, and took it again in resurrection.

If righteousness is imputed to me because He died for me, holiness and a new righteousness are imparted to me because He lives in me. And that is the great message we have to bear to men today. There are thousands of men who will hardly thank you for the doctrine of forgiveness unless you can tell them there is salvation from the slavery of sin.

And yet once again. A man will say, I saw the vision, and I knew I was a sinner. I have received the value and am forgiven by the Cross. There has been imparted to me its virtues, and I am enabled to do the things I could not do.

But what other forces are there? Must I fight this battle alone? And there comes the crowning declaration of the evangel, never to be put off as a second subject, as a second blessing, or anything else. Right here in line is the coming to man of Jesus by the Holy Spirit, that Spirit to be the Paraclete, the Advocate, the One Who in the life is the dynamic, the force that shall produce the coming victory in the man.

What then shall I say to the men to whom I preach the evangel? One thing only, Submit to the Lord Christ.

And if a man does that what then?

Then the Lord Christ by the Holy Spirit will make over to him the value of His dying, will communicate to him the virtue of His living, will pour into him the victory of the indwelling Spirit.

These three things are the necessary consequence of the submission of life to His Lordship. Men will not be saved by understanding the atonement. Men will not be saved by explaining the mystery of resurrection. Men will not be saved by explanation of the mystery of how the Spirit comes. They will just be saved by yielding to the Lord Christ. In the moment of yielding he makes over to them all the virtues and values.

I have attempted to speak of the New Testament evangel. Let me close by saying, the evangel is the only one that meets the essential needs of human nature in any age. It is ageless. You cannot say it is old or new. It must be zealously guarded from addition or subtraction. To add conditions to the evangel of the New Testament, or to curtail it, is to make it value less and vicious.

To deprive the evangel of any note is to make it inoperative. If you are preaching an evangel with no vision of the Lord Christ, it is emasculated. If you are preaching an evangel without the value of His death, it is anaemic. If you are preaching an evangel with no virtue in it, it is sentimental. If you are preaching an evangel with no victory, it is hopeless.

If we have this great whole, the vision of the Lord, the value of His cross, the virtue of His life, the victory of His indwelling by the Spirit, you have yet to find me the city, the village, the nation, the people, the man, or the child, that will not have such good news as they are waiting for, and apart from which there can be no hope.

The Church Evangelistic

Evangelism apart from the Church is impossible.

Christ was, and is the one Evangelist. He now fulfils His great work of proclaiming the good tidings through His Body, which is the Church.

In the four Gospels we have a picture of Christ, and at the opening of His second treatise Luke makes use of words which indicate for us the character of the Gospel narrative, and suggest that of the book of the Acts of the Apostles.

"The former treatise I made, O Theophilus, concerning all that Jesus began both to do and to teach, until the day in which He was received up." That sentence reveals to us the character of the Gospel story. The "former treatise" is the story of the beginning of the doing and the teaching of Jesus.

The latter is therefore by inference the story of the continuity of the doing and teaching of Christ. In the Gospel Jesus is seen—to use His own suggestive word—"straitened" until His baptism should be accomplished.

In the book of the Acts of the Apostles the same Jesus is seen no longer straightened, for the passion-baptism is accomplished, and He risen, ascended, enthroned, has come into new relationship with men by the Holy Spirit, to continue His work through the Church by the Spirit. Consequently, the evangel proclaimed by Christ in measure during His life, is proclaimed by Christ in fullness through the Church by the Holy Spirit in this age.

Evangelism apart from the Church is apart from Christ, and is therefore no evangelism. There can be no evangelism save that of Jesus Christ, and that can only be spoken by Christ Himself through His people by the Holy Spirit. Anything calling itself evangelism which is not the outcome of that new life of Christ, realized in the soul of men, and spoken through men by Christ, is not evangelism.

Unattached and unauthorized evangelism, even by individual members of the Church of Christ, is to say the least, unwise, and not the most fruitful of permanent results. I do not desire to criticize unkindly any movement that acts independently of the churches, although I do not hesitate to say that I have grave suspicion of everything that boasts that it is un-denominational.

I have a very great love for everything that is inter-denominational, which is quite another matter. But all unattached, freelance work, unauthorized and ungoverned by the Church, is not the best work possible, and tends to disorder and confusion.

We must hold to the very highest doctrine of the Church, or our evangelism will be weak and one-sided. Believing therefore that the relation between the Church and evangelistic work is all important, we will carefully consider the Church as to its creation, its nature, and its purpose.

The New Testament deals with the Church in two ways, as Catholic and as local; the whole Church of the Living God, and a church in any given locality.

Sometimes I am asked what church I belong to. When I reply, I am a Catholic Churchman, I have seen people look surprised. Yet that is exactly what I am. Catholic means universal. The Catholic Church is the whole Church. Such a phrase as "Roman Catholic" constitutes an absurd contradiction of terms. If Catholic, then not Roman. If Roman only, then by no means Catholic. That is equally true of the term "Anglican Catholic."

The New Testament deals with the whole Church, but it also deals with the local church. The word Church is used sometimes of the whole Church of God, and some times of a church in a given locality, as in Ephesus, in Corinth, in Thessalonica, in Philippi.

So far as the records reveal, the Lord only twice in the course of His public ministry referred to the Church. He used the word Church once in its catholic sense, and once in its local sense, so that the general New Testament uses of the word harmonize with that of Christ.

The first occasion was when Peter had made the supreme confession of the Messiahship of Jesus, "Thou art the Christ." At that parting of the ways the first half of our Lord's work was accomplished. He had taught a little group of men, the nucleus of His Kingdom, that He was the Christ, the Anointed, the Messiah of God. And then He immediately commenced to teach them a new thing, to bring them into view of the path way through which the Messiah should accomplish the purpose of God.

He began to talk to them of the Cross, but before mentioning the Cross He said to Peter, "Thou art Peter, and upon this rock I will build My Church; and the gates of Hades shall not prevail against it." That is a perfect, final, and all-inclusive declaration concerning the Church.

First, "Upon this rock I will build My Church." Secondly, "the gates of Hades shall not prevail against it," not one thing repeated, but two distinct facts about the Church.

I think we have too often read the passage as though the Lord said the same thing twice over. But if you follow the figure carefully, you will find that Jesus was absolute Master of metaphor. There was no blunder, and no intellectual inaccuracy in the figures He used. "On this rock," that is the declaration of the impregnable strength of His Church against the attacks from without. "I will build," that is an affirmation of the certainty of its perfection and completion.

But what follows? The same thing repeated in another form? By no means. "The gates of Hades shall not prevail against it." That does not mean that the Church is impregnable against attack, but rather that she is unconquerable when she goes forth to attack. An attacking force never carries its own gates up to besiege a city. If Hades is contemplating an attack upon the Church, it will not carry its gates with it. The idea is not that Hades will attack the Church, but that the Church will attack Hades, and as she does so, the very gates of Hades will yield before her.

Thus we have two declarations about the Church by the Master; she is built by Christ on the rock, and when she goes forth on the conquests of Christ, she conquers all intervening foes, and finally the last enemy, the very gates of Hades, shall yield to her. She shall conquer through life, through death, and unto the endless ages. That is the Church I belong to, the Church impregnable, unconquerable, marching out in perpetual triumph into the ages beyond. That is Christ's estimate of the Church.

On a subsequent occasion Jesus mentions the Church again. "If thy brother sin against thee, go, show him his fault between thee and him alone; if he hears thee, thou hast gained thy brother. But if he hears thee not, take thee one or two more, that at the mouth of two witnesses, or three, every word may be established. And if he refuses to hear them, tell it unto the church; and if he refuses to hear the church also, let him be unto thee as the Gentile and the publican." That is the church local.

It is impossible to tell to the whole catholic Church anything between your brother and yourself; but it can be told and it ought to be told to the local church if that brother is refusing to listen. It is a perfect picture of the church's discipline. The church is to be so constituted, a fellowship of souls in Christ, that the wrong doing of one is felt by, and affects the whole; and the purity of the entire Church must be maintained, even at the cost of the excommunication of a brother who persists in wrong doing.

Thus we learn from the words of Jesus, that the Church is the building of Christ on the rock, that the Church is the aggressive force which Christ leads to ultimate victory, that the Church within herself is a fellowship exercising discipline, caring for her own internal life, and able to exercise final and Divine authority in the case of all those in membership. These things are true of the catholic Church, and also of the local Church.

From these first uses of the word in the New Testament it is at once seen that the local church is a model of the catholic Church, that all the truths concerning the catholic Church are true in measure and in degree of the local church, and if we would understand what the function and the force of the local church is, we shall have to attempt to get a vision of the function and the force of the catholic Church.

Now as I pass from these words of Jesus, one or two words concerning the use of the word in the Acts of the Apostles will be in order. In the second chapter of the Acts of the Apostles, and the forty-seventh verse, "And the Lord added to them day by day those that were saved," the word church is inserted in King James Version, It is not in the original text. Its introduction is of the nature of exposition, and translators almost in variably break down when they attempt exposition.

The statement thero is that, "the Lord added together them that were being saved and the translators thought it must be "added to the Church." Seeing the word Church was not there in the original, the English and American revisers altered it, and put "added to them," that is, to the disciples. That also is only true in a secondary sense. The thought is that He added them to

Himself. Of course it is true that when He adds a man to Himself, He adds him to the Church.

Through the Acts of the Apostles the word Church is used sometimes of the catholic and sometimes of the local church, and the local is always treated as a part and model of the catholic. The actual word ecclesia is used of the congregation of Israel in the wilderness once.

In the nineteenth chapter the word is used in the purely Greek sense, "Some therefore cried one thing, and some another: for the assembly was in confusion. . . . But if ye seek anything about other matters, it shall be settled in the regular assembly. . . . When he had thus spoken, he dismissed the assembly." That word assembly is ecclesia. I am not suggesting that the translation is improper. I think it is wise that the word assembly is used on this occasion.

What was the assembly here referred to? It was the gathering together of the members of one particular trade. It is the first record we have, so far as I know, of a trade union meeting, and the word assembly indicates the truth. The reference is not to the great promiscuous crowd which was congregated to see what was going on, but that particular and select number, bound together by a common purpose under a common impulse.

The Greek word is there used in its simplest form. It means a called out assembly. It is the assembly of the silversmiths, and it is the assembly of the town government. That is the word ecclesia, in its simple etymological intention.

That word has been taken hold of by the Christian fact, and has become the great word for the Church. And it means very simply, an assembly of people, called out, selected from the rest.

In the letter to the Ephesians we have a picture of the Church in these wonderful words, "There is one body, and one Spirit, even as also ye were called in one hope of your calling; one Lord, one faith, one baptism, one God and Father of all, Who is over all, and through all, and in all." There is nothing in all the New Testament that is more wonderful in its revelation of the nature of the true Church.

Notice first the apostle describes the Church, as "one body." What is the body? Christ and every believer. Not the believers without Christ. The body includes the Head. Of course if we speak of the Head and the body, then for the single moment we mean by the body, all except the Head; but in the statement "there is one body," in this passage the apostle is taking in the whole fact, Christ Who is the Head, and all members. "One Spirit," that is the life of the one body, the intelligence of the one body, the emotion of the one body, the will of the one body. "He that is joined to the Lord is one Spirit," so that the whole body of the Church is one with the Head, and the Head is one with the body, and that one unifying Spirit of God, in Christ and in all believers, creates the one body. One dominating life that of the Spirit, in Christ and in the believer, unifying Christ and the believer, and all believers with each other, because all are united to Christ.

"One body, and one Spirit, even as also ye were called in one hope of your calling," that is to say, there is one calling for Christ and the believer, for the whole Church which is the body. In the former part of the epistle that calling is declared to be that of showing to the ages to come the grace of God, and teaching the principalities and powers in the heavenlies the manifold wisdom of God. That will be the work of Christ and His people forever.

One body, Christ and all the members. One Spirit, filling the whole body up to its last reach. One calling, the eternal calling of Christ in union with the Church, and the

Church in union with Christ. This is a general statement concerning the organism, the life, the calling of the Church.

The apostle next shows how individual members become members of the Church, how the units enter this living unity. "One Lord," the Object of faith; "one faith," set upon the one Lord; "one baptism," the baptism of the Holy Spirit, that unites the faithful soul with the living Lord. That is the whole process.

The first note in the evangel is that of the Lordship of Christ. Jesus is Lord by virtue of the splendour of His character, by virtue of the victory of His Cross, by virtue of the power of His resurrection. That "one Lord," is presented to the soul as the Object of faith. The answer of faith to the vision of the Lord is the whole of human responsibility. That is the "one faith." Its nature is that of believing on Him, or receiving Him as Lord. It is the act of the will in surrender. That act of faith is responded to by the "one baptism," that baptism of the Holy Spirit whereby the soul believing on the Lord is made a member of the Lord Himself.

Thus the individual enters the Church. The one Lord is presented to him. He believes. The Spirit baptizes him, and he is a member. The human responsibility is belief, the Divine answer is the baptism of the Holy Spirit whereby that man is merged into the Christ life, and becomes a member of Jesus Christ. "One Lord, one faith, one baptism."

Thus is He building His Church. Man cannot admit into the catholic Church. No one is admitted into the Church by water baptism, nor by vote of a church meeting, nor by the decision of a session.

A person enters the Church when the Holy Spirit baptizes him into Christ. All the other things may be necessary in order that the discipline of the local church may be maintained.

There ought to be solemn recognition of some kind when a man joins the outward and visible church, but all such matters are outward and visible recognitions of the inward and invisible facts. The only condition on which any person should be admitted to a local church is that evidence is given of membership in the catholic Church by the baptism of the Holy Spirit.

Once again, "One God and Father of all, Who is over all, and through all, and in all." That is the last fact of the sevenfold unity. It indicates the glorious realization of the purpose and plan of God in His government of, operation through, and union with the ransomed society.

This great Church of the firstborn is being built, and as yet man has never seen it. We see parts of it, but the scaffolding is all about it yet; and sometimes it seems as though there were more scaffolding than Church. But when He comes, all the scaffolding will go; and the glorious Church of the firstborn, made up of ransomed souls baptized into the life of Christ, the great entity and unity through which God will manifest Himself to ages and to principalities, will be revealed in all its radiant splendour.

Let us now think of the local church in the light of this. Every church is, as is the catholic Church, an assembly of those submitted to the Lordship of Christ. That is the gate, that is the entrance, that is the foundation fact.

A local church is therefore an assembly of souls submitted to the Lordship of Christ. That does not tell all the story, but it gives the key to the whole truth. Everything else follows, and to understand that, let us go back to our evangel.

The first note is that of the Lordship of Christ. Men submit to that Lordship by believing on Him. Then not only do they see the vision of the Lord, but share the value of His death, and the virtue of His life, and the victory of His presence.

In the fifth chapter of Romans we see how these things are realized within the Church in the living members who are baptized into union with Christ. The tenth verse, "For if, while we were enemies, we were reconciled to God through the death of His Son, much more, being reconciled, shall we be saved in His life."

The seventeenth verse, "For if, by the trespass of one, death reigned through the one; much more shall they that receive the abundance of grace of the gift of righteousness reign in life through the One." "Reconciled by His death," "reign in life."

Now as an aid to memory let us take three words, reconciled, regenerate, regnant. These words mark the truth in the case of every individual believer. The individual believer submitted to the Lord ship of Christ, is reconciled to God by the value of His death, regenerate by the virtue of His life communicated, regnant[1] by the indwelling Christ through the Holy Spirit.

Now believing that a church is an assembly of such persons, what results follow? Every church is intended to be within itself a manifestation of all the purposes and the facts of the Kingdom of God. A church is an assembly of persons, who in the power of the indwelling life of Christ, realizing the ideals of Jesus, obey the teaching of Jesus, and take part in the activities of Jesus.

It is here where perhaps the Church has most sadly failed in the past, and where the failure of the Church today is most apparent. We have too largely looked upon the negative side, which has to do almost exclusively with such facts as constitute the saving of the individual from

---

[1] Regnant – Reigning or ruling

sin, and from punishment. These are most important facts.

But the great society of God, vitally one, essentially one, socially one, aggressively one, where is it at the present hour? The Church ought to be a society accepting the ideals of Jesus, and realizing them in the power of His life; consequently, a society of people obeying the moral code of Jesus, and therefore a society of people manifesting to the world the breadth and beauty and beneficence of the Kingship of God in and through Jesus Christ. Is that what the Church is? That is what the Church ought to be, for that is the Divine intention.

But someone will say, what has all this to do with the evangelistic Church. And the very fact of the question reveals the weakness of the hour. The Church has largely failed in evangelism because the Church has not realized within her own borders the force of her own life.

We ask how is it that the masses refuse to listen to her evangel, and are treating her in so marked a degree, with contempt? Because the masses see perfectly well that she is not obedient to her own Master's ideals, and does not realize His purpose.

That is the severest criticism, and it ought to make us blush, and hide our heads with shame, that the Church is not fulfilling her Master's ideals. The evangelistic Church is the Church which shares Christ's life, and in the power of it obeys His law, and thus manifests Him to the world. Thus alone can the Church engage in His work, and carry out His enterprises. When the Church realizes and manifests her Lord, in her personal membership, and corporate capacity, then, and then only is she doing His work, the work of seeking and saving the lost. That is the evangelistic Church, and that is the true Church of Jesus Christ.

The purpose of the Church is certainly that of con serving the life of the saints, but this only in order that every saint, and all the saints, may be strong for carrying out the purposes and the work of Jesus Christ. "Ye shall be My witnesses," not witnesses as talkers merely, but evidences, credentials, demonstrations, proofs among men. The only Church which is truly evangelistic is the Church which realizes within her own borders all the will of her Lord and Master Jesus Christ.

Strength of spiritual life always issues in the manifestation through the Church to the world of the facts of the Kingship of God in Christ, and the power of Jesus Christ to deal with all the things in human life that are contrary to the mind and will of God.

The Church is to be aggressive, capturing men, fighting against wrong, urging everywhere and always the claims of Jesus Christ, and this she can only be as within her own borders there is realized the purposes of God.

In conclusion, the evangelical Church is necessarily evangelistic. There are some things so patent they ought not to need stating. Yet there seems to be a prevalent idea that it is possible for a church to be evangelical and not evangelistic. It is not possible.

A friend of mine in the ministry, a man of whose scholarship and whose devotion there can be no doubt, talking to me about evangelistic work, accounting for his own lack of interest said, "Well I am profoundly evangelical, but I am by no means evangelistic." There would seem to be many who take that view. Let me say to you, my brethren, that this is an absurd contradiction of terms. No man is truly evangelical unless he is evangelistic also.

What did my friend mean? He meant that he held the evangelical doctrines of our holy faith, but he was not interested in the specific work of winning men to Christ.

Now what are the foundation doctrines of our holy faith? Evangelical faith affirms the death of Christ was rendered necessary by the ruin of the race, and that it is God's provision for man's salvation. It moreover declares that His life is at the disposal of men for their new life of holiness.

Are we evangelical? Do we believe that Jesus died in order that He might save men? If not, then we cannot claim to be evangelical. But if we do, can we seriously assert that holding the doctrines, we are yet content to do nothing for the men for whom Christ died? Knowing that we have the deposit of truth, the great evangel, equal to the salvation of men, are we careless about making it known?

Sometimes one reads an advertisement which declares a sure and certain cure for cancer has been discovered. A man so advertising is wholly despicable. In the first place because the assertion is a lie, but secondly because if it is true, he is a rogue to hold for purposes of personal gain a secret which should immediately be given to the world for the cure of that awful disease. And a man tells me he is evangelical, he holds the truth about salvation, and is thankful to God for the salvation of his own poor miserable soul. I deny it. If the Cross of Christ in his own life has meant deliverance, cleansing, purity, that consciousness will drive any man out into evangelistic work and effort.

Evangelism demands a Church, and wherever the Church of Jesus Christ is, there is an instrument for evangelistic work, because there is a company of men and women in whom the evangel has won its victory, and through whom it is manifested as a life, and pro claimed as a message.

Let me say to all ministers, you will find you must have your church act with you if you are going to do any evangelistic work. And to church members, it is no use wasting breath in the criticism of a minister because he is not doing evangelistic work. Let the Church fall into line. One of the first missions of the ministry will be to bring his church into sympathy, and that will often need a great deal of common sense and patience.

No church ought to be allowed to exist that has not added to its membership by confession of faith. If a church is existing only by letters of transfer, it is time the doors were closed, and "Ichabod, the glory of the Lord has departed" was inscribed across them.

This evangelism must begin in the churches. The churches themselves must be turned back to the work of evangelism.

We are trusting too much to organizations outside the Church. It is in the Church the work must be done. We shall have to travail in birth for the souls of our own people. When in our own church life all the forces of the Christ life are operative without hindrance, then men will be brought under the sound and power of the great and glorious evangel. May God make all our churches, churches after the pattern of the catholic Church, "one body, one Spirit, one calling," and "God over, through, in all," moving to His purpose, accomplishing that purpose through the Spirit of Jesus Christ.

The Evangelist

The doctrine of New Testament ministry lies wholly within that of the Church. The ministry serves the Church under the Lordship of Christ.

That is not to say that ministers are servants of the Church in the sense of obeying the Church. They do serve the Church but they obey the Lord Christ. From that statement two initial truths are to be deduced and remembered:

First, the ministry has no right to lord it over God's heritage; and secondly, God's heritage has no right to lord it over the ministry. I have of set purpose used Peter's phrase. Writing to the elders and the bishops he says, "neither lording it over the charge allotted to you."

The word "charge" there is kleros, the word from which we derive our word clergy. According to Peter, the whole Church was the clergy, and bishops were men who were to serve the clergy, and not lord it over them. Every believer is in the priesthood, and the whole Church is the clergy, and yet within the whole Church there is a distinct ministry.

Our present subject is concerned principally with that section of the Christian ministry indicated by the word evangelist. But in order properly to understand the function of the evangelist we must take time to set that particular aspect of the ministry in relation to the whole. There is too often a measure of friction between the evangelist and those who are exercising other gifts of the ministry, and this friction acts in two ways.

Pastors and teachers sometimes entertain a feeling almost amounting to contempt for evangelists. The evangelist on the other hand, very often manifests a contempt for pastor and teacher.

Now this is all utterly false; contrary to the spirit of the New Testament, contrary to the spirit of love, contrary to the spirit of wisdom, contrary to the Spirit of God. If we may but see the inter relationship of these gifts, that a man is in the ministry, not by his own choice, but by the choice of the Holy Spirit, and that the work of each is not contradictory to the work of the rest, but complementary rather, then we shall be a long way towards understanding the true place of the evangelist, and making for him his proper place in the work of the Church of Jesus Christ.

"He gave some apostles, and some prophets, and some evangelists, and some pastors and teachers, for the perfecting of the saints, for the work of the ministry." This is the reading of the King James Version, and we have interpreted it as though these gifts were bestowed in order that those receiving them might perfect the saints, and do the work of the ministry. As a matter of fact, what the apostle meant was that these gifts are bestowed on men in the Church, in order that they may by their ministry perfect the Church, so that the Church may do the work of the ministry.

The fullest fact of ministry includes the whole Church, and the men within it who have received special gifts, have received them in order that they may perfect the Church to its work of ministry. The translation of the Revisers makes this much clearer, "He gave some apostles; and some, prophets; and some, evangelists; and some, pastors and teachers; for the perfecting of the saints, unto the work of ministering"

"He gave some apostles." The specific work of the apostles was the perfecting of the doctrine, the fundamental basis of teaching.

"He gave some, prophets." The work of the prophet was the perfecting of the forth-telling, the declaration of the truth.

"He gave some, evangelists." The work of the evangelist is the perfecting of the number of the Church by calling men into relationship with Christ.

"He gave some, pastors and teachers." Their work lies wholly within the Church, and is that of perfecting the character of the members of the Church in order that the whole Church may be perfectly equipped for its ministry.

These are the true orders of the Christian ministry. These are the fundamental and spiritual orders, and we must recognize them if there is to be any fulfilment of the whole function of our ministry.

But now let us enquire how a person in the Church becomes a minister within the Church.

Let us turn to Corinthians, in the first letter, chapter twelve. Here we have a chapter that always ought to be read side by side with this fourth chapter of Ephesians, on the subject of Church order. In that chapter you will find that the apostle, beginning a section concerning the spiritualities, deals first with the Lordship of Jesus, and then with the ministry of the Spirit of God, and as a sub-section thereof, with the gifts bestowed by the Spirit.

He is dealing with gifts far larger than those of the ministry to which he refers in Ephesians. In the course of his argument he makes a statement of vital importance, that the Spirit bestows these gifts upon "each one severally even as He will." In Ephesians the same principle is declared, that "He gave some, apostles; He gave some, prophets; He gave some, evangelists; He gave some, pastors and teachers." The whole emphasis of the truth is that capacity for ministry in any form is a gift, and it is a gift bestowed by the Head of the Church through the Holy Spirit according to His own pleasure.

Therefore no man can choose to be a minister of Jesus Christ, as any man may choose the profession of medicine, or of law. No man ever really enters the Christian ministry in the deep spiritual sense of the term, save as he receives a gift from the Head of the Church by the Holy Spirit which perfectly equips him for the work he has to do.

We are hearing a great deal in these days of the dearth of men entering our theological seminaries.

I have been asked if I would not urge upon young men that they should give themselves to the ministry, urge them to adopt the ministry as a calling in life which is high, and holy, and beautiful. And my reply always is, I dare not urge any man. No man can enter the ministry of his own will and choice. The only way in which a man can possibly enter the ministry is when the Holy Spirit of God bestows upon him a gift from the Head of the Church. By that gift he is made a minister of Jesus Christ. Nothing short of that makes a minister, and that being so, nothing can prevent his being a minister, except his own disobedience to the heavenly calling.

I would very solemnly urge young men to consider well whether or not they have not had the gift and the calling, and are refusing it. Has there come upon your soul somewhere, somewhen, a burning passion to preach the Word, a great constraint, a sure conviction that you can preach it; and have you allowed some secular calling, some material advantage to persuade you that you can still be a good Christian and make money? It is at the peril of your soul you stay there. If once the gift is bestowed then "woe" is that man if he "preach not the Gospel."

Notice in the next place that these gifts refer to special spiritual qualifications for the doing of special spiritual service. What is a gift bestowed upon a man? What is the gift of the apostle, the gift of the prophet, the gift of the evangelist, the gift of the pastor and teacher?

I do not mean what is the specific value or the distinction between these, but what is the underlying quality in each? What is a gift? The gifts are certainly not such as may be designated natural endowments. They are spiritual quantities and qualities, bestowed for the doing of spiritual work.

A man receives the gift of an apostle. Then in him there is a spiritual force, a spiritual vision, a spiritual fitness that his brethren have not, which fits him for doing a distinctly spiritual work, the work of the apostolate. So with all of them. The gift is a spiritual qualification.

But while it is true that the gift is bestowed, and is not merely a natural endowment, it is also perfectly certain that the Spirit of God never bestows a spiritual gift for service except upon men who have natural endowments that will enable them to use it. There is nothing in the economy of God out of joint and out of place. There is perfect harmony between God's first creation and the bestowment of special spiritual gifts.

The new birth does not mean the death of everything essential and noble in the first birth, but its life. So also when God bestows the gift of the apostle, or the prophet, or the evangelist, or the pastor and teacher upon a man, the gift will be bestowed upon men who have natural aptitudes and fitness and endowments for their work. A young man in my church tells me God has called him to preach. Then I immediately give him opportunities to preach.

I find him an occasion in the Mission Hall, or in a cottage; and in oversight with me there will be my brethren in the diaconate[2], and they will hear him, not critically, but with the solicitude of a great and passionate desire to help him. And if after a little while we find that the man has no

---

[2] Diaconate - the office of deacon, or a person's tenure in it.

natural endowment I would say to him in love and in all honesty, my friend, you have evidently made a mistake. God has never called you to preach, or you would be able to preach.

We have been making the terrible mistake of putting a man through the theological seminary, and when he has completed his course we find, and he finds that he is not a preacher, and so he writes essays to the end of time. Essays are excellent things, but the writing and reading of them is not preaching.

We must find the men with natural endowments and the spiritual gifts. If a man has that twofold equipment, and is responsive to the heavenly vision, you cannot stop him preaching, and you cannot stop his preaching with power. The gift is a spiritual quantity and quality, bestowed upon a man having natural endowments.

The gift of the pastor and teacher will be a spiritual quality of appreciation of truth bestowed upon a man who is a born teacher and a born shepherd. The gift of the prophet will be an appreciation of truth in its application to the needs of his age, bestowed upon a man, who if he is not a preacher must be a speaker somewhere or other.

It is affirmed that men with absolutely no gift of speech, receiving the spiritual gift have become great preachers. Personally I have never known such a case. I was told in England some years ago by a dear man who held very strongly that all spiritual power in service was spiritual merely, that, there was no connection between man's natural capacity and the spiritual gift, and the instance cited was D. L. Moody, and I was told he had no natural gifts of oratory, that everything he had was the spiritual equipment. I am not undervaluing the spiritual equipment, but if D. L. Moody had gone into politics instead of preaching, you would have found that he would have swayed vast audiences, and that he was a man of natural endowment.

A gift is a spiritual quantity and quality bestowed by the Head of the Church at His own will through the Holy Spirit upon those who are naturally endowed to receive it. That is the fundamental truth concerning the vocation and the force and the power of the Christian ministry.

Let us now notice the inter-relation of these gifts. The apostle was the first messenger. The work of the apostle consisted in the proclaiming of truth first, and then in the committal to sacred writings of the truth.

It is written in the Acts of the Apostles that the early disciples "continued steadfastly in the apostles' teaching." In that phrase we have the indication of one part of the work of the apostolate. I am inclined to say the gift of the apostolate is still conferred under certain circumstances for specific work. At the birth of all great missionary movements there has been an apostle, a first messenger, one with a specific gift to go forth and tell at the beginning the doctrines of the Way.

Then we have the work of the prophet. The peculiar and distinctive note of prophetic utterance is that a man who is a prophet foretells the truth from God without any reference to the pleasure or anger of the people. This is the prophetic note. You find it in the old prophecies. "Whether they will hear, or whether they will forbear." The prophet is not an evangelist. The prophet does not come down into personal dealing, and constraint of individual lives. The prophet is a man whose voice is lifted in an age, pouring out truth, compelling the age at least to hear it. Whether it will obey or not is not his responsibility. That is the characteristic note of the prophet in all dispensations. And God has never been without prophets in this Christian era.

The evangelist is a name signifying a man who tells the glad tidings always with a view to constraining the man who listens by the evangel, to that of which the evangel bears testimony. I am inclined to think that the opportunity of the evangelist is today often made by the prophet; that in prophetic utterances and prophetic ministry there is an arousing of conscience and inquiry, and to that the evangelist comes with his personal and individual message of the Lordship of Christ; the value of His Cross; the virtue of His resurrection; and the glorious victory of His indwelling. And the evangelist is therefore the one who in the name of the Church tells men and women outside how they may come inside, declares the glorious glad news of the infinite Gospel.

As in response to the message of the evangel, men crowd to the Christ, owning Him Lord, receiving the value of His death, the virtue of His life, the assurance of victory, then the pastor and teacher begins to teach them, and train them, and to watch over them.

There are two words that mark the work of the pastor and teacher; overseer, and pastor. He is one who watches, and feeds the flock of God.

John Milton, when speaking of false pastors, and their failure in the ministry de scribes them in a most remarkable phrase. He speaks of them as "blind mouths." And he says, "The hungry sheep look up, and are not fed." It is a terrible indictment, and that because it is scriptural. It appears a contradiction in terms, "blind mouths." It is not so, for as Ruskin points out, Milton brought together the two facts in the work of the pastor and teacher.

His first work is to watch over the flock, but Milton says he is "blind." His second work is to feed the sheep, but Milton says instead of doing that he is trying to be fed himself, he is a "mouth."

Let no evangelist think that the pastor and teacher who year by year patiently feeds the flock is not doing God's work because he is not doing that of the evangelist. And let no pastor and teacher think that the men passing over the country like a flame of fire, proclaiming salvation and constraining men to acceptance, are sensational merely.

Oh this great Church of Jesus Christ, if we could only realize it, with its great gifts; the apostle, the first messenger to the new region; the prophet, the perpetual voice proclaiming truth, the evangelist, the perpetual voice calling men to the Christ, the pastor and teacher, instructing, leading, guiding, and culturing the saints.

But I must leave that larger outlook. I have at least said enough to show the place of the evangelist, and to show there is no antagonism between the work of the different orders.

I once heard W. L. Watkinson, one of the most wonderful preachers in England today, with a marvellous gift of sanctified satire, say in a great congregation of ministers, "The pity is we do not understand each other." He continued, "I go to one man in the regular pastorate, and I say to him, 'What do you think of these special men' and he replies with a curl of his lip, 'Sensation.'': And then I come to a special man and I say to him, "What do you think of that quiet man down there' and he says, 'Oh, stagnation!' "And that tells the truth of the attitude too often indulged in against each other.

In the light of this great truth of the complementary nature of the gifts we ought to recognize the fact that every man in the ministry, while he will have one specific gift above all others, will yet have sympathy with all the rest, for I still believe that the Holy Spirit confers gifts of this order upon the Church, giving some prophets, some evangelists, some pastors and teachers.

Happy indeed is that church whose ecclesiastical order will allow it to make room for a man to exercise the gift God has bestowed, and unhappy is that Church who wants each of its ministers to be something of a prophet, and something of an evangelist, and something of a pastor and teacher, and thus making him something of each, makes him the whole of nothing. We want room for the orderliness of the Spirit of God in our ecclesiastical arrangements.

But now where this is established, and we see the inter relation of these gifts, and how there is no conflict but perfect harmony where the whole Church and ministry is under the dominance of the Spirit, we may turn to the specific gift of the evangelist.

In the New Testament only two men are definitely spoken of as evangelists. Philip is called an evangelist, and in the final charge of Paul to Timothy, he says "Fulfil thy ministry, do the work of an evangelist." It is at least significant that the two men who are called evangelists are in entirely different circumstances, and suggests as I think, the two types of the evangelist.

Philip was a man at large. He was not definitely in charge of any Church, nor was he, as I believe, set apart by any apostolic function to his work. He was an evangelist, prepared by the impartation of a qualification for telling the Gospel, to tell the Gospel. He moves from place to place. He goes to Samaria, then he speaks to the individual eunuch, and is caught away to Azotus. Then we find him moving up through Caesarea, at last settling down, his children coming up after him, and uttering the same great Gospel. That is one evangelist as I see him in the Acts of the Apostles.

The other is a man, who is in oversight of the Church at Ephesus, placed in oversight through certain difficulties arising there, and the letter of the apostle is written to instruct him in his work.

I am inclined to think that the more special work of Timothy was that of the evangelist, moving from place to place. But Paul saw the necessity of a certain oversight at Ephesus, and sent him there. And he writes to him of his charge, the church; and instructs him as to how he shall take over sight; but the last thing the apostle urges is that he shall not forget that though he is now in oversight of the church through certain ecclesiastical difficulties, he is to fulfil his ministry, and do the work of an evangelist.

It is at least significant that these two men are described by the term evangelist, the one moving from place to place, and the other settled in oversight of a church.

Having simply referred to that by way of illustration, in order that we may understand that the evangelist may be a man called to move from point to point, or he may be a man placed by God in the oversight of a church, I want to speak of this gift itself.

I have said of all these gifts that they are spiritual quantities and qualities. There is no specific description in the New Testament of either of these gifts bestowed. We may however safely argue from the work the nature of the gift.

A man who receives the gift of the evangelist is one to whom there is given a clear understanding of the evangel, a great passion in his heart results from the clear vision, a great optimism fills his soul, born of his confidence in the power of Christ to save every man; and growing out of that passion and that confidence a great constraint seizes him to tell somebody, to tell everybody the glad news of salvation by Jesus Christ.

Those peculiar qualities are not found in all men called to the ministry. Every man will have sympathy along these lines. There are however other forms of spiritual gifts, as we have seen. But where this is the all-consuming fire, there you have an evangelist.

Granted that a man has the gift, on what line is he to be trained for the exercise thereof? He must be trained in theory and in practice, and the training of theory and practice must go side by side during the whole time of his preparation for the exercise of his gift.

Wherever possible I would give a man the profoundest and fullest academic training possible, but I would put each theological seminary in, or not far from a great city, and I would send the theological students down into the slums to teach and to preach.

There are men advising us to save men by education, and the latest thing I hear suggested is salvation by psychology. This kind of suggestion is however, always confined to theory and does not get beyond the book in which it is discussed. A good many books issue from the press which would never see the light if while the man was thinking out his problem he had to go into the slum district or suburban quarter for the definite business of saving men.

A man must be trained, but the man who has this passion must exercise it, he must use it. A man who has this constraint must not be hindered from going out to exercise the gift, or else the gift within him will burn down to cinders and ashes.

While exercising his gift, let him be trained in every way. The evangelist ought to be a man, a whole man, a man who is to be a perfect instrument for that perfect Gospel he is called to preach. He is to train physically, to train mentally, and above everything else, to train spiritually. We have no right to think that while all the other vocations of life, of the lawyer, of the doctor, of the business man, demand preparatory hard work and training, that we can successfully put untrained men into the work of the ministry.

If God takes hold of a man He has called to the work, and it is really impossible for him to obtain training, and he becomes a veritable flame of fire, that is no reason why other men should shirk training, and slip carelessly into the work of the evangelist.

The very magnificence of your Gospel, the very majesty of your work demands that you should take time, take your whole being, and attempt to make it a fit instrument for the proclamation of the great Gospel.

I would like to say a good deal about physical training. If a man is going to preach this evangel, he has no right to trifle with his physical powers. My body is to be the temple of the Holy Ghost, who through me, will proclaim this evangel, and I am to see to it so far as I am able, that in all its powers it is an instrument fit for the Master's work.

And so with the mind. Ignorance is not a qualification for evangelism My dear young brother, are you looking forward to an evangelistic ministry? Then I plead with you, gird up the loins of your mind, and obtain all the knowledge possible.

No single branch of knowledge is out of place to the man who is going to do the work of an evangelist. You may gather illustrations from all sciences, from all literature, and if you are only living close to the centre, and close to Christ, you will see light gleaming and breaking everywhere.

Don't hurry through training in order to do this work, but while the training goes on, let there be exercise al-the while, and through the process you will gain in strength, and become presently an evangelist proclaiming the message with the vigour of physical strength, with the acumen of mental equipment, and with the dynamic of spiritual force. Such are the men for whom the world waits at this moment, for the preaching of this great Gospel of Jesus Christ.

Then if this is the gift and the training of the evangelist, what is his work? The evangelist is to go forth and preach the Lordship of Christ, preach Him as Lord until men in the presence of His Lordship become conscious of their own failure. Then begins the great commission of declaring to them that by His Cross salvation has come to them, that all they are not, they may be, and all they are, they need not be, that the things they would not be but are, can be cancelled in blood, the things they would be, but are not, they may be by life in the Spirit. Oh this is a great message, the evangel of the Cross.

But is the proclamation all? By no means! The evangelist must constrain men to obey. There must be that wonderful wooing note that breaks men's hearts, and sweeps them to Christ. That is the final and most remarkable note of the real evangelist, by which he constrains men. Not merely the declaration of the evangel, not merely the announcement of the Lordship of Christ, and the declaration of the Cross, but the ability to take hold of men, and compel them to Christ.

Of course some worldly critic will call this personal magnetism. That however is not all the truth. It is the constraint of the personality of Christ through the personality of the consecrated men which wins.

Think of the great evangelists, stern men very often, and yet their sternness always melted into tears. Every great evangelist has been of that nature. The late Robert W. Dale of Birmingham, England, greatest of our theologians said to me, sitting in his study one day, "I think I have only known one evangelist that I felt had the right to speak of a lost soul." And I said, "Who was it?" He replied, "It was D. L. Moody, and it was because he never spoke of the possibility of a man being lost without tears in his voice." He turned from fiery denunciation of sin into quiet plaintive tearful heart-broken constraint. It is the great equipment. It is the great secret.

If all this be true, what manner of man is the evangelist to be in his own character? First of all, he must himself be a credential of the Gospel he preaches. It is no use my preaching the Lordship of Christ unless I am loyal to Him. I may eloquently describe His Kingship, I may with acumen defend Him against the attacks of others; but if my life is not loyal, my eloquence is sounding brass, a tinkling cymbal, a blasphemy and an impertinence.

And the man who preaches the Cross must be a crucified man. You may preach the Cross and it is nothing but a Roman gibbet unless you preach it from yourself. It is the crucified man that can preach the Cross. Said Thomas "Except I shall see in His hands the print of the nails ... I will not believe." Dr. Parker of London said that what Thomas said of Christ, the world is saying about the Church. And the world is saying to every preacher: Unless I see in your hands the print of the nails I will not believe.

It is true.

It is the man who is at the end of himself, who has got to the end of reputation, and the end of earthly ambition, the man who has died with Christ, he it is that can preach the Cross of Christ.

And yet more. Not only loyal to His Lordship, and not only realizing the power of His Cross, but revealing the glory of His resurrection in a life rising above the things of this life, triumphing every day; not merely the man of the Cross, but the man of the Easter morning.

Are you, dear brother mine, preacher of the evangel, are you an Easter morning man? It is not the Cross only. It is the Cross and resurrection. Have you come to resurrection by the way of the Cross? Is the radiance of its glory on your brow? Is the song of an assured victory in your heart? If you are doubting, you cannot inspire faith. If you are not sure how this thing is going to turn out, no one will be persuaded. You must be the man of certainty, a man on the resurrection side of the grave, the old life behind.

You remember the old story of a boy flying his kite. He could not see it. A gentle man passing said to him, "What are you doing?" "Flying my kite." "Oh but," he said, "you cannot see it." "No, but I feel its pull." It is the man who feels the pull of the unseen things that is going to preach this Gospel, and the only man who does that will be the man who by the way of the Cross, has come out into the resurrection life.

And consequently the evangelist is a man not only preaching the possibility of victory by the indwelling Christ, he is in himself truly optimistic in the power of personal realization of victory. Pessimism paralyzes power in evangelistic preaching; but this great optimism of the indwelling of Christ is a perpetual power.

And all this means the necessity for unceasing vigilance. The man who is to be an evangelist, the voice of the Church, proclaiming the glad news, how zealously and jealously he must guard the gift committed to him. What personal examination and correction are necessary if this work is to be perfectly done.

Oh the subtle and insidious foes of the minister, sloth, ambition, pride, distraction, these are the things that spoil us. My brothers, how we must guard against them. How the evangelist needs to live in perpetual fellowship with God. How he needs earnestly to devote himself to the hard working, brain-sweating study of his message. And how the evangelist needs to be perpetually on the watch for souls.

Let me gather up and conclude. Sympathy with the evangelist is in every man gifted by the Spirit, though all may not have the specific gift. The varieties create the harmonies. Harmony is a concord of differences. So whether you have that specific gift or no, you have sympathy with it if you are Christ's own minister. At least keep that sympathy alive and warm. Don't let anything freeze it out, paralyze it.

My special word is to you, my brothers, perhaps to a few only, whom God has called to this special work.

Let your spirit be carefully guarded. And yet more strongly let me say that you as a witness in the Church, having the gift of the evangelist, ought to be able to inspire everyone you meet, men and women in your Church, with the sympathy and passion that consumes you. That is your first and greatest work even as an evangelist.

And as there is no calling more wonderful than that of the evangelist, therefore none demands more in cost and in toil.

And now this final word to those in whose hearts there burns the sympathy. By your prayer, by your co-operation, by your determined attempt to sweep everything out of the highway, help these men who are called and gifted for the proclamation of the message.

And if in the pastor of your church you have discovered a man in whose heart there is this great passion and constraint, driving him to win souls, oh, I beseech you, don't hinder him, don't bind him, don't prevent him, don't demand that he shall put that which is a gift of evangelism into its wrong use of taking care of you, but rather in your co-operation with him, catch the same spirit, carry on the same great glorious work.

Thus all of us in measure, while some by specific equipment, may be evangelists of the Cross.

The Evangelistic Service

This is the phase of our subject which personally I should prefer to omit. I freely confess to a fear of the study of methods. I am well aware that such a study is necessary, but I am always a little afraid lest we should attempt to press into some ready-made method, the infinite Spirit of God.

"The wind bloweth where it will, and thou hearest the voice thereof, but knowest not whence it cometh, and whither it goeth, so is every one that is born of the Spirit." These words of our Master have very wide application. They indicate the spontaneity of the work of the Spirit. No man can tell whence the wind cometh, or whither it goeth. No man can foretell the line along which the Spirit of God will operate toward the accomplishment of the Divine purpose.

It is nevertheless true that no man will make the wind his servant unless he learns the true method of answering its law. The wind blows where it will, but if I want the wind to be my servant, and propel my boat across the sea I must know how to construct my boat and my sail to catch the wind.

And so while the Spirit of God is the one Worker, without whom nothing can be done along the line of true evangelism, it is nevertheless true that it is important that we should discover those methods with which He works most easily and naturally, and in proportion as we do this we shall be able to co-operate with Him in all His great work and purpose.

In dealing with the conduct of an evangelistic service, it must be distinctly understood that I would not attempt to compel every man to use one method, and above all, I would not attempt to suggest that I have discovered the final or best method by which the Spirit may work.

I want to speak first of all of the place of evangelistic services in the course of the regular ministry, and then of the work of evangelism at special seasons in the life of a church or community.

The presence in our congregations of those not actually and personally submitted to Christ, must always create the necessity for such service.

Nothing can be more paralyzing to the life of a minister himself, or to the congregations that assemble regularly to hear him as he preaches the word, than that he should come to think, or should so preach as to make his people think, that definite decision for Christ is not important in every individual life. There is a very great peril along that line to all of us in the work of the regular ministry.

I am very thankful to be able to speak to you from the standpoint of twelve years' experience in the settled work of the ministry. I know exactly what it is to face a congregation Sabbath after Sabbath. There is nothing more full of delight than that kind of work, but there is a danger that we take too much for granted about the people to whom we preach, and if we are not careful we shall drift into the opinion that because these people are attending services, therefore there is no need for the direct appeal of the evangel to be made to them.

We must ever remember that it is necessary that every individual person should come into personal relationship with Jesus Christ.

We must remember that no child is born a Christian. That is not for one single moment to enter into any discussion as to the question whether or not the children of Christian people are born within a covenant. I believe they are, but they are not born Christians; and whereas I very strongly hold,—and my own life's experience is the most remarkable testimony to the truth of the fact,—that where a child is born of Christian parents, and is trained in a Christian home, the actual acceptance of Jesus Christ as Lord by that child is likely to be natural and simple, without revulsion, without earthquake shock, soft as the kiss of morning on the brow of Nature, sweet as the passing zephyr over the fields of flowers, yet there must be definite submission, and no child because born of Christian parents, is therefore a Christian.

In all our preaching we need to remember that the dear children of our own members, coming with them to worship—and there is no fairer sight to my own eyes than that of seeing father and mother and children sitting before me Sabbath after Sabbath—must each one for himself and herself, at some age of understanding and discretion, yield their own life to Jesus Christ, or else they can never be Christians.

Now with that conviction in the heart of the minister, he will at once see how there must be in his preaching, even though he be a pastor and teacher principally, a desire for the salvation of these, and there must be occasionally some message, some appeal, some opportunity given to those who sit under his ministry, to make an immediate decision and a definite confession of Jesus Christ.

No man can have as the burden of his preaching the Lordship of Christ, whether the special quality be that of the prophet, or that of the evangelist, or that of the pastor and teacher, without bringing to the consciences of those who hear him a conviction of sin.

In the first of these lectures I laid special emphasis upon the first note of the evangel, the Lordship of Christ. It is the great theme of preaching. It is the message of the prophet to his age. It is the message of the evangelist to the individual. It is the message of the pastor and teacher, to his people. The prophet pro claims that Jesus is Lord over all the affairs of men.

The evangelist proclaims that Jesus is Lord in the realm of the salvation of the individual. The pastor and teacher insists upon the Lordship of Christ in the actual life of the believer. And no man can preach that Lordship in all the spaciousness of its meaning, without those who hear him coming into the consciousness of sin.

Now wherever as the result of the preaching of the Lordship of Christ, conviction of sin results in the con sciences of those who hear, there at once is created the necessity for the proclamation of the way of salvation, or in other words, there is the opportunity for the evangelistic service.

Therefore, I submit that the minister of Jesus Christ ought occasionally to hold meetings where he urges immediate decision, and gives the opportunity for the same.

We must not be led astray from the essential work of the Christian ministry by imagining we have some gift which liberates us from responsibility about the decision of the men and women who listen to us. There is no gift that does not include within it something of the evangelistic necessity, of urging the claim of Christ upon individuals.

I hold no regular ministry is complete in which there is never an opportunity for immediate decision on the part of those who are brought into contact with the fact of the Lordship of Christ, and who hear the evangel of salvation.

As to time and season, my own conviction is that in the work of the regular ministry in the vast majority of cases it is not wise to decide that on every Sunday night there shall be an evangelistic service. There are exceptions to this rule. The local circumstances must always decide.

In the Moody church of Chicago, where Sunday by Sunday there is gathered together a promiscuous crowd, no Sabbath evening passes without an evangelistic appeal, and without decisions for Christ. Some persons imagine that because it is done there, it ought to be so everywhere. That by no means follows.

Neither do I think it wise to hold an evangelistic service at stated intervals. That is too mechanical an arrangement. The pastor who is living in fellowship with the Spirit of God, and who is seeking to receive his messages direct from God, will discover when the moment has come in which he must declare the evangel, and make his appeal. That is the occasion for the evangelistic service.

If I may refer to my own experience as a pastor, I have gone on from Sunday to Sunday, sometimes for one or two months with an evangelistic service after each evening service.

On the other hand, there have been periods when only once in the month or perhaps twice, such services have been held, and sometimes months would pass with no such service. I never went to my pulpit knowing whether I would have such a service or not. I went with a burden and a message, and having endeavoured to lead and train my church in co-operation with me, they were never surprised if I had an after-meeting. If I did hold one, I found my officers and workers ready to do the necessary work.

There are a thousand men who have not the specific gift of the evangelist, who yet are able to do evangelistic work occasionally as opportunity occurs. There are a thousand men who have not the particular quality that draws to their church the promiscuous and large multitude, but who nevertheless, are in the ministry by the gift and appointment of God, and their special work will be that of preaching regularly to a congregation composed very largely of the same people, but into which strangers will constantly be coming.

There is no congregation made up of saints, consequently there will be in all congregations an element of those interested but not submitted, and the minister must ever have on his heart the burden of such people.

A great many ministers say to me; we don't feel we can conduct evangelistic services like that. How shall we do it?

First of all, by the use of your natural endowments. There are men who have remarkable powers of persuasion at an election, who yet say they cannot urge men to decision for Christ. If you have influenced a man to vote as he ought to vote for the good of the country, you should be able to win a man for Christ.

A man in the ministry of Jesus Christ, whose heart has been touched with the Spirit of God, must feel the compassion of the heart of Christ towards men, and must feel the winning and drawing power of the Christ over men. If a minister has no compassion for men, no yearning for souls, no knowledge of what it is to travail in birth for the souls of men, he should search his own heart and life, and see what it means, for there must be something wrong between him and his Lord, or that compassion and power of constraint would most certainly be there.

As to the conduct of an after-meeting. The first thing necessary is that the minister should preach so as to make one necessary. It is no use conducting an after-meeting after any sort of preaching. If decision has been urged in the preaching, then I cannot help thinking that if in the power of the Spirit an appeal be made for immediate response, it will be realized.

Two or three years ago it was my privilege to take part in the simultaneous mission arranged for by the Free Church Council of England. Some people will tell you that mission was a failure. That is only partially true. I am quite prepared to admit that it did not succeed in any large extent, in reaching the vast masses of the unchurched people.

There were exceptions of course, but both in London and the provinces there were whole regions, residential regions very often, as well as slum regions, which were hardly touched, at all.

But the movement was a glorious success in that it aroused in the hearts of hundreds of pastors an interest in evangelistic work, and turned them to evangelism in their own churches.

The provincial mission which I conducted was held in the Town Hall of the city. There were united in that mission all the Free Churches. God greatly blessed the services, and many were brought to Christ.

The last meeting I held was with the ministers, a conference in which they asked what they could do to take up and carry on the work. I suggested that on the next Sunday night every man, whether he had ever done so before or not, should preach to his own congregation with the distinctive and avowed purpose of persuading many of them whom he loved, but who as yet had not yielded to Christ, to yield to Him at once.

To this they agreed, and on that next Sunday night every minister preached to his own people an evangelistic sermon, held an after-meeting, and through all the city men and women were saved. I believe that every minister who would prayorfully hold such a service in his own church, and among his own people, would have actual and definite results.

Now as to evangelistic services at special seasons. Such seasons may arise in some individual church, or in some union movement among the churches. I do not propose now to discuss the union movements. I am not discrediting them. I thank God for all of them which are so much blessed in my own country, and in this. For the splendid work being done by Dr. Torrey and Mr. Alexander I thank God perpetually.

But what I am principally interested in is a new devotion to evangelistic work in our churches, and consequently I want to confine myself very largely to the special mission of evangelism in the church.

In the work of a faithful ministry there will come special seasons when the minister and office bearers alike will have borne in upon them the conviction that the time is ripe for harvest. The movement may begin with some woman who prays, and keeps on praying quietly and alone, making no talk about it, until a conviction that God is beginning to work takes possession of the whole church. That is the occasion for the work of the special evangelist.

Very many feel that the minister himself is the true man for the work. It may be so in some instances, but it is more fitting in the majority of cases that the minister should seek for some man to co-operate with him, whose gift is specifically that of the evangelist.

Now as to method and management. When the church is conscious of imminent Divine visitation there must be the most careful and watchful preparation. It should begin in the gathering together of the church for united prayer. I think that when the church is conscious of Divine visitation, of the movement of the Spirit of God, there need be no indecent hurry. Nothing is lost by a time of waiting, during which the church is gathered together for solemn preparation by consecration and intercession.

Then there must be systematic preparation as to the needs of the whole neighbourhood. If a church in a district or neighbourhood is going to hold a series of special meetings, that is the moment in which that church stretches out in actual endeavour to reach the whole neighbourhood.

Every house in the neighbourhood will receive invitations to the services, and it will be seen that an invitation shall reach every person, not once or twice, but a dozen times before the services begin. That is very detailed and technical I know, but it is along such lines of hard work, and consecrated prayerful preparation that the greatest blessings have come to services held in connection with individual churches.

During the course of the meetings every member of the church should be a worker. It may be urged that that is a counsel of perfection which can never be carried out. At least let it be a counsel of perfection, and let every church attempt to realize it.

It may be objected that it is not necessary that every church member should be a worker. And yet nothing is more important. There are many kinds of workers wanted in connection with evangelistic meetings, house-to-house visitors; Christian men and women in the choir to sing the Gospel; Christian men as ushers; specially trained and qualified enquiry room workers; and beyond all these, a band of men and women, who unable to help in any of the ways indicated, shall labour together with the rest, in earnest pleading prayer.

The church membership should be called together, and the burden of this matter laid upon them in the spirit of prayer. Then let arrangements be made. Finding out what each is fitted for, allot "to every man his work."

The importance of house-to-house visitation is very great. Let the visitation be courteous and kind, and yet insistent as to the claims of Jesus Christ, devoid of arrogance, but characterized by a winning courteous manner. Let that be done time after time, until it shall be impossible for any human being in the neighbourhood of the church to say "no man careth for my soul."

As to the singing. If there is one thing not wanted in evangelistic work it is a number of unconverted men and women to lead the singing. Christian men and women are needed, who in all their singing show the tender and matchless power of Jesus Christ, and they should be gathered out of the church.

Then as to the stewards and ushers. Are we not sometimes a little in danger of forgetting the importance of them? The way a man is met at the door and shown to his chair, may decide him for or against God. The way a man is welcomed or repulsed may attract him to Christ or drive him from Christ.

In all such special services there should be the greatest care taken that those attending should be welcomed by those who manifest the love of Christ. You may have all your angular, peculiar, crotchety sidemen when the church only is there, but you want the men of gracious strength, and tender heart, and loving welcome, and genial face, and sweet Christian life to welcome men into the house of God when you are going to urge them to decision for Jesus Christ.

And finally the enquiry room workers. Let me utter here a solemn word of warning.

Make your enquiry room secure against the intrusion of any person unknown.

Let anybody have the right to enter the enquiry room, and all the fads and fanatics of the district will be there first. I was jealously, zealously careful to guard my enquiry room against the intrusion of any person not known to myself.

That means there must be preparation by the minister of his workers, and there ought to be an enquiry room class in which he shall meet a chosen band and instruct them in the method of dealing with souls. These need appointing and arranging for with great wisdom and care.

If the membership is not exhausted by these appointments, then all the rest can pray.

I am greatly impressed today as I meet with men whom God is using, and find their experience coinciding so closely with my own. I crave today more than I ever did in my life, with a greater longing than I ever felt, to know that men and women are praying for me.

In New York recently three men came to me, and these three men looked into my face and said, "For five years we three have prayed for you every day by solemn covenant." I cannot tell you what it meant to me. If our evangelistic work is going to be a success we must get our people regularly and systematically to pray.

Epaphras agonized in prayer. Now it is not given to everyone to spend long hours in prayer. Thank God for the men and women who can do it. God does not mean everybody should do that.

But we can form the habit of prayer, so that we can pray here, there, anywhere, everywhere. Let the members band themselves together to pray.

It has often been pointed out that it is a remarkable thing that when Paul preached on Mar's Hill, there were few if any converts, but when Peter preached on the day of Pentecost thousands were swept into the Kingdom of God; and it is an interesting question why in the one case so few, and in the other so many were attracted and influenced.

No one would like to suggest that Peter was more abandoned to God than Paul. Peter preached in the midst of a company of praying men and women, and

Paul did not. And account for it as you will, go into the mystery and philosophy of it as you will, the fact remains that the Holy Spirit of God works more easily in the atmosphere of praying men and women than without them.

Then the combined business acumen of the church members should be consecrated to this work. Oh, when will all the business ability in the church be consecrated to the work of the Church? Some men think that they need their business ability for their business, and that it is enough to give a check to the church.

If a man is offering for sale something that he wants to make profit out of for himself, he will push it in front of your eyes wherever you go. I cannot travel any distance without seeing the virtues of some soap extolled under my eyes wherever I look. If I could only get hold of the business acumen, and turn it into account for the Kingdom of God.

I don't quite like the comparison, but I am going to use it. When the Church begins to run the business of Jesus Christ like the world runs the business of selling soap, we shall do something.

I will tell you a story out of my own experience. I went at one time to conduct a series of special services in a district in England. I was to be there for two weeks. One of the officers wrote to me just before I went, and he said, "Our chapel has been renovated, and very beautifully renovated, and we are afraid the crowds may spoil it, and we are going to have the services only for one week." Oh, the shame of it! The preservation of paint of more importance than the salvation of souls!

Let the business men of the Church recognize that they are in business partnership with Jesus Christ, and let them apply all the push and go which they use in their own business to the business of the Kingdom.

That should be so always, but specially in the time of the special mission. Such preparation is mechanical, but it is the mechanism through which the Holy Spirit of God may do His work.

The work of the evangelistic mission in our churches first demands all our consecrated endeavour. If we attempt to do it in any other way, we shall fail as we deserve to do.

If for instance we say we will hold some special services, and then issue two hundred and fifty bills, four inches square, and open the doors and imagine we have done everything, we are demonstrating our unbelief in our own enterprise, and the world is very apt to measure the importance of those things by the standard of the Church's estimate of their value.

We must put into the work of saving men and women sinew and brain, and muscle, and blood, and then we shall begin to move the world.

Finally, I want to say something as to the actual conduct of an evangelistic service, whether it be the occasional service in the regular work of the pastorate, or whether in the special series.

In an evangelistic service the whole conduct of the service must be conducive to the one business of winning men.

I begin with the smaller matters first.

The physical conditions must be remembered. The building in which the evangelistic service is to be held must be one in which it is possible for people to be physically comfortable.

There was a good man in Sheffield, England, named Tom Graham, remarkable in his success in winning souls, who used to say something not elegant in expression, but perpetually true, "I never knew a man saved with cold feet."

It is of prime importance that we attend to the physical conditions. The building must be such as people can at least be comfortable in, and by being comfortable forget the physical and attend to the spiritual. As long as a man is conscious of the physical it is very hard for him to attend to the spiritual. The building must be properly warmed and ventilated. The physical conditions must be of the best.

The next point of importance is that those who enter the building to an evangelistic service should be welcomed. The caretaker and the ushers must be chosen with great care if this is to be so. Then accommodation must be provided, and so far as possible those coming must be courteously seated, and attended to. We must in love make men feel that they are more welcome to this service than they ever were in a saloon or theatre.

Then further in the evangelistic service the general tone of the proceedings should be carefully guarded. There should be an absence of merely stilted dignity on the part of the minister and the office bearers of the church.

D. L. Moody once said that dignity was not one of the fruits of the Spirit anyhow. If a poor man comes into the church and is patronized, the chances of winning him are greatly reduced.

And yet the tone should not only be free from stilted dignity, it should be free from all undue frivolity. Nothing should be done by speaker, singer, or anyone else for the sake of simply raising a laugh. I am sorry for the man who lacks a sense of humour, but humour should be the play of summer lightning, clearing the air, and not the degradation of the pulpit into an entertainment, in which the main object is to make people laugh.

The tone should be that of a reverent gladness, the hymns pulsating with hope, the attitude, of every man taking part in the work that of one who believes in God, and in the possibilities of the man that has come in. Reverent and hopeful in all things let the true evangelistic service be.

And once again. The whole of the service in the hands of the evangelist should conduce to the one matter in hand, of winning men for Christ, the singing, the Scripture, and prayer, and the sermon.

I do not believe that it is wise in an evangelistic service that the evangelist should hand the conduct of the singing over to any second man. In the actual service he should select his own hymns, such as will lead up to his subject, and such as will appeal to the people on the line thereof.

I would have half an hour's singing before the service proper begins, under the charge of the director, but the moment I come to the platform as the evangelist, I want to select my own hymns. I don't want a hymn sung absolutely out of harmony with anything I am going to say. There needs to be this harmony.

So also with the matter of the Scripture reading. So also with the prayer prayed. An evangelist will be very careful about whom he asks to pray. It is a great mistake to take hold of the Rev. Mr. So and So, who does not believe in evangelistic meetings, and get him to lead in prayer in order to enlist his sympathy. I don't want to do him good just now. I am after this sinner here, and I want the man to pray who knows the way into the secret place, who knows how to get at the heart of God.

All these things are important. I do not think we can afford to miss a single detail.

And as to the sermon. In an evangelistic service it must be one aimed at the capture of the will for Jesus Christ.

Different congregations will demand different methods. One method of presenting truth will appeal to one class of the community, and quite another method will be necessary for another class.

Thomas Chapness says that the most remarkable text on how to be a soul winner is the text, "I will make you fishers of men." I once heard him speak on that text, and in the course of his sermon he said, "A fisher is very careful about his bait. If I want to catch a codfish, I fling them out a bait as big as a clock weight, and they swallow it. But if I am going for salmon I have a fly, and whip the stream with delicacy and art"

There are some preachers who will appeal along the line of the intellect and reason. There are men caught on the flood tide of emotion. But back of the intellect and emotion is the citadel, the will, and it is for that the preacher strives.

Whether he captures the will through the intellect or through the emotion depends upon the persons addressed and on the preacher; but the supreme business is to appeal to the will, and to bring it into submission to the Lordship of Christ.

The business of the evangelist is to get a verdict for Jesus Christ there and then. To the realization of that everything else must therefore be subservient in the sermon.

The preacher's literary reputation, the preacher's rhetorical reputation, yes, the preacher's theological reputation.

The evangelist in the preaching of the evangelistic sermon will not be principally occupied with literary form, or rhetorical expression, or even of theology as such. His business will be to get that man for Christ, and when that is remembered, the sermon will get its true tone, its true quality.

One other word. The true evangelist will be very careful to avoid the possibility of a passion for numbered results spoiling his message.

I sometimes fear lest the desire to have large statistical returns may tend to make a man make the way of salvation unduly easy. I think there is a danger. We have been preaching 'Believe' and we have not sufficiently said 'Repent repent repent' and we have still to preach this truth, that unless a man will turn to God from idols, then his faith though he boast of it, is dead and worthless.

There is no question of precedence. The quality of faith must be that of repentence, and the dynamic of repentance must be that of faith, and when we urge upon men that they believe on the Lord Jesus, we must say that belief means submission to the Lordship, and that means turning from every other lord that has held dominion over the soul.

We must not lower the claim of truth as presented to the people. Therefore, the evangelistic sermon must be as carefully prepared as any other sermon. We cannot dare to imagine that we have the right to face a great crowd of people, and declare the evangel unless we have taken solemn time to know the evangel, its terms, its content, and its message to men.

When some of our best trained men, the most highly equipped mentally turn to aggressive evangelism, then we shall have the most successful evangelists.

A word about the after-meeting.

I feel very strongly that the best method of conducting an after-meeting is that of making it an after-meeting rather than a continuance of the first meeting.

That runs counter to many ideas. Let every man be fully persuaded in his own mind. Personally I do not like an after-meeting at which any are unwillingly present. I ask that all those who would like to stay behind do so. I never make an appeal (or very rarely under pressure of circumstances) until I have given an opportunity to everybody to go who desires to do so.

It is sometimes said that by such means we miss so many men upon whom the Spirit of God has put His constraint. I do not believe it, and I would rather have a dozen people constrained, convicted, and converted, than a hundred caught in some emotional movement, in which movement there was no real depth of conviction and result.

The after-meeting is to give men and women an opportunity to decide for Christ and confess Him immediately and openly.

Here occurs the place for enquiry room work. There is no sacramental virtue in an enquiry room. The enquiry room is simply for enquiring souls to come that they may be intelligently dealt with about the spiritual perplexities. And that makes necessary the training of enquiry room workers.

You cannot deal intelligently and correctly with a hundred at once. Every case has an individual problem, and there are two words that cover the ground of such work, and these are the words diagnosis and direction.

By diagnosis I mean that the intelligent enquiry room worker will take hold of the case and find out where the particular difficulty is. It is not at all wise to say, 'All you have to do is to believe. The difficulty in each case must be discovered, and there needs careful, spiritual, proper training, in order that it may be done.

When the difficulty is found out, then there must be the quiet clear pointing of that soul to Christ. Then whether in the after-meeting or in the enquiry room, there is a point where preacher or worker must stand aside, and leave the soul with God alone.

I have seen people go with their Bible to an enquirer, and say, 'Now do you see that verse?' 'Oh, yes' 'Well, can you read that verse?' 'Oh, yes.' 'Read that verse' and that person will read that verse, and then the worker says 'Now do you believe that?' 'Yes, I believe that.' 'Then you are saved.'

Now we have no business to tell any man he is saved. There is a point where we have to stand aside and let God and the man deal alone with each other. We can help, lead, point, counsel, warn, plead, but at last regeneration is the coming of God to the soul that comes to Him, and we have to draw aside and leave the individual to God.

I close as I began. I do not like lectures on methods, and I pray you, receive what I have said only as I have attempted to show principles, and not as I have attempted to lay down rules.

But the great and supreme matter is this, that every church of Jesus Christ ought to have in it evangelistic work going on regularly or periodically, and add to its membership by such as are led to Christ individually and directly.

The Present Opportunity

It is always difficult to measure correctly the times in which we live. It has been said that no man can write the history of his own times.

Consequently, it is not easy for one to understand the spirit of his own age, and yet those who are called to lead must know something of that spirit; indeed, it is one of the essential qualifications for leadership.

When the tribes came up to make David king at Hebron, it is said of the children of Issachar that they "had understanding of the times, to know what Israel ought to do," and immediately afterwards it is further said, "all their brethren were at their commandment." That is to say, the men that led were the men of Issachar, and all the rest of the tribes were willing to follow their lead.

That was the qualification of leadership, "men that had understanding of the times, to know what Israel ought to do." To any of us God calls to leadership, and I do not mean only conspicuous examples, but those called into the ministry of the Word in any form, one of the prime qualifications is an understanding of the times.

It is pre-eminently difficult to form an estimate in spiritual matters. There is a wide application in the words of Jesus, "The wind bloweth where it will, and thou hearest the voice thereof, but knowest not whence it cometh, and whither it goeth: so is everyone that is born of the Spirit."

There are things about the blowing of the wind we do not know, so also with regard to the spirit of the age. And yet the Master rebuked the men who did not understand their own age. He said, Ye hypocrites, "When it is evening, ye say, it will be fair weather, for the heaven is red. And in the morning, it will be foul weather today: for the heaven is red and lowering. Ye know how to discern the face of the heaven; but ye cannot discern the signs of the times."

Recognizing both the difficulty and necessity then, I want to speak first of the spirit of the age, and then to ask, have we an evangel that meets the demand?

The spirit of an age is not always to be discovered at first glance, or by a merely casual survey of the field. Much that is about us is the issue of a past, and the true spirit of an age is not to be defined by the general consensus of opinion, but by the single voices which are beginning to sound, which for the moment are startling and full of surprise.

If I casually survey the age, the first thing which I notice is its materialism. We are cursed by materialism.

Commercial prosperity has seemed as though it would grind under its heel all spiritual life. That is the general outlook. Yet if a man should say that the spirit of the age is that of materialism, he has missed the deepest note. He has not heard the deepest voice, but has taken the casual outlook. A general survey is not what we need.

It was said of President McKinley that he was a great statesman, because he had the faculty of putting his ear to the ground, and listening for the things that were coming. It was a remarkable capacity. A man who knows how to listen for the new voices, and see the fresh visions is the true statesman. In the words of the Bible he is a man "who has understanding of the times," and knows what the people ought to do.

We don't want to be led astray by the clamour of the mob. We want to listen for the new voices, the voices which are forming public opinion.

If that be understood, I want to say three things.

I think that the spirit of the age is characterized first, by a revolt against materialism. That is the very opposite of the first impression. Yet I believe that to be the note which is sounding clearly at the present moment.

And next there is abroad a new passion for the practical. Call it altruism, utilitarianism if you will. I prefer the other phrase because it is more simple.

And the third fact is that there is a great sense present in the hearts of men today, of some coming visitation. These three notes mark the spirit of the age in which we are called to live and serve; first, a revolt against materialism; second, a new passion for that which is practical; and finally, a great, mystic, mysterious sense of some coming visitation.

First of all, I suppose having referred to materialism, and then having declared that there is a revolt against materialism, it is perfectly fair to ask me to demonstrate my statement.

One of the evidences that there is a revolt against materialism in the air is the marvellous and astounding growth of Christian Science[3].

As to Christian Science itself I hold it to be characterized by an absence of the Christian, and an ignorance of science. But here is a great movement, and it is fair that we should ask, what does it mean?

I have travelled in your railways over eighty thousand miles, and visited cities, and touched all sections of the Christian ministry, and there is hardly a place where Christian Science is not successful.

It is not only that they gather into their fold fanatics or people characterized by neurosis, but some of the sweetest and best Christians have also gone over to them.

---

[3] The Church of Christ, Scientist was founded in 1879 in Boston, Massachusetts, by Mary Baker Eddy, author of Science and Health with Key to the Scriptures, and founder of Christian Science.

What is the secret? Christian Science stands for two things: the negation of sin, and the affirmation of the spiritual.

That is an attempt to get at the heart of it. It says, there is no material, everything is spiritual. Matter does not exist. It is a mental fault, a mental miscalculation to imagine you have matter. Thus they emphasize the spiritual, falsely emphasizing it as we believe, and absurdly too, but this very emphasis of the spiritual has been the attraction of a people tired of materialism.

The materialism of the past said, matter is everything, but today Christian Science says, no, matter is nothing, the spiritual is everything. The argument we hold to be ridiculous and absurd and laughable, but the underlying principle is the thing that draws the multitudes, a reaffirmation of the spiritual.

And then the negation of sin. Here is where we supremely join issue with Christian Scientists. They are calling something Christian which denies atonement, because it denies sin. Any theory that denies the sin of man, and denies the Cross of Christ is something to be dreaded.

And yet even though they deny the atonement of Christ, they endeavour to get rid of sin by denial. I do not hesitate to affirm that if the Christian Church had only been true to the Gospel of spirituality, and the Gospel of holiness, there would have been no room for Christian Science. And yet the presence of it in our midst is evidence of a revolt against materialism, and though it is but a will-o-the-wisp, that dances among the quagmires, men would rather have the will-o-the-wisp than the dense black darkness of materialism.

It is a sign of the times.

But still far more striking is it that the affirmations of science at the present hour most remarkably demonstrate the truth that the age is characterized by revolt from materialism. Huxley, Spencer, Tyndal, Darwin twenty-five years ago denied the reality of anything except matter.

We heard much of the atom, of the protoplasmic germ, of the fortuitous concurrence of atoms, and these were given to us as the final solution of which man was capable, of the whole riddle and mystery of the universe.

Lord Kelvin, the Nestor[4] of British scientific thought, perhaps the most remarkable living man of science, has said, that "Science positively affirms creative power, and makes everyone feel a miracle in himself." He says, "It is not in dead matter that man lives, moves or has being, but in the creative and directive power, which science compels them to accept as an article of scientific belief."

The latest scientific pronouncement of the age is that there is something at the back of matter, that there is a spiritual force behind.

Science has not yet gone far enough to define, but it has absolutely abandoned the position of twenty-five years ago, that all that is, is the accidental coming together of atoms. Darwin's evolutionary theory has passed. The evolutionary theory has not passed but has come to stay. It is probably true in certain realms. But the evolutionary theory of Darwin is not held by reputable scientific men today. That some germ of truth lies within the theory there can be no longer any doubt, but we are now coming to see that while the evolutionary theory may have an application to the material realm, it does not account for spiritual life at any point. And the scientist is acknowledging it.

---

[4] a king of Pylos in Peloponnesus, who in old age led his subjects to the Trojan War. His wisdom and eloquence were proverbial.

Two very remarkable books have recently been issued. First that of Professor James of Harvard University, entitled, "Varieties of Religious Experiences."

This is a book written not from the standard of a Christian man, a book written not by a professor in a Christian Theological Seminary, but by a professor of psychology, plainly and simply upon the basis of scientific study of the psychological problems of life.

He has gathered up all kinds of religious experiences, and after carefully and systematically examining his data, has made his deductions. Let me read you one sentence from the part of the book in which the Professor gives his conclusions.

He claims they are scientific conclusions based upon an examination of data. "We and God have business with each other, and in opening ourselves to His influence, our deepest destiny is fulfilled." Here is a scientific testimony that thousands of men are reading in this land today. Men that call themselves scientists, take this book up, and they read that after examination of the experiences of men, the professor has come to this twofold conclusion, first that man has dealings with God, and that human life can only fulfil its deepest destiny when man is submitted to the government of God.

The influence of such a deduction by so eminent a scientific thinker is bound to be that of creating a revolt from materialism in the minds of thousands of the thinking youth of our colleges and universities.

And yet once again, there has issued from the press, since Prof. James' book, a book by Frederic W. H. Myers. The history of Myers is an interesting one. He was an Oxonean, and a pronounced High Church man and during that period of his High Churchism, he wrote the poem of "St. Paul," to me at least one of the most exquisite pieces of poetry in the English language.

After that he passed into agnosticism, reverent agnosticism, never attacking Christianity, but declaring himself to be unsure. There he lived for years, became interested in the work of the Psychical Research Society, of the phenomena of spiritual existences as they manifested themselves in ordinary life, and outside the church.

He has left two volumes, published after his death, the title of which reveals the subject. "Human Personality, and its Survival of Bodily Death." Such a book is received by scientists, they will read this book, and they will not all agree that he has proved his case.

But as Myers says, twenty-five years from now no reputable scientist will question the fact of the resurrection of Jesus Christ from among the dead. In the next twenty-five years we have to speak to people in whom there will be a reawakened sense of the reality of the spiritual.

There is nothing more encouraging than this, that in the world of purely scientific investigation there is a reaffirmation of all the things we stand for.

The next note of the age is a passion for the practical.

I need hardly stay, in speaking to American audiences, to prove the truth of this. You have a passion for the practical, for you have no respect for ancient things.

Americans have no respect for institutions merely as such, and I confess I have the profoundest sympathy with them.

It is the altruistic spirit which governs this great people, and it is in the vanguard of humanity at the present moment.

The cry today is for an ethical and social Gospel. Everywhere men are crying for a social and ethical Gospel, for something that touches all needs of men's lives. There is a passion everywhere for something that conditions actual life, and affects the details of every man's doings. It is a true passion. The passion for the practical is manifesting itself in England in a new antagonism to Christianity.

Robert Blatchford is writing the most definite articles of attack on Christianity. He is rousing the whole of the pulpits in England to consider and answer them. So strong a paper as the "British Weekly" has thought it necessary to devote space to answering these attacks.

What is it this man is attacking?

He is attacking the miraculous and supernatural elements in Christianity, the virgin birth of our Holy Lord, and His resurrection.

Why?

Because Christianity fails to do what he thinks she ought to do; and consequently this very antagonism of his is a new sign of the passion for the practical.

And lastly there is a sense of coming visitation, of which we hear from all sides and from divers voices.

Mistakes of interpretation there may be, but the general fact is recognized. Men everywhere are looking for something, they hardly know what.

Thus I hold that today the age is characterized by revolt against materialism, by a passion for the practical, and by a sense of daybreak at hand.

Now let me ask, does our evangel fit the needs of the age? Have we any need to find a new evangel, or what shall we do? I submit that the evangel of Jesus Christ exactly answers the need created by the spirit of the age, for it is a protest against materialism, and an assertion of the variety of the spiritual; it is practical, or it is nothing; and the visitation that is to come must have as its essential notes the very evangel committed to us to declare.

The evangel is exactly in harmony with the spirit of the age in its revolt against materialism.

What is the Gospel that we have to preach?

What are the notes of the Gospel?

The first note in the evangel of Jesus Christ is the assertion of His Lordship. The preaching of the Lordship of Christ will answer this cry for spirituality.

Kelvin has affirmed the Divinity of creation or the Deity at back of creation. Jesus long ago stood among the flowers and birds, and said, God clothes these flowers, and feeds these birds. The last scientific assertion synchronizes with the simple statement of the Nazarene long years ago, that at back of the flower, and bird, and everything, is God.

Dr. James says, "We have dealings with God." That is the last affirmation of psychological science. Listen, "Seek ye first His Kingdom, and His righteousness, and all these things shall be added unto you." That is the answer of our King. The last affirmation of psychological science harmonizes with what He taught.

Frederic Myers in his posthumous work affirms in this day human personality to be stronger than death, to exist after the death of the body, that man does not cease to exist when his body ceases to exist. That is the whole declaration of two great volumes. Listen. "Be not afraid of them that kill the body, and after that have no more that they can do."

In neither of these cases did Jesus Christ defend what these men are affirming. They refer to them as discoveries. He referred to them incidentally, as established verities.

What this age needs is to show that Jesus is Lord in the intellectual realm, and that the last things scientists are saying, are in harmony with the things Jesus Christ said centuries ago.

He was not the half-educated and half-ignorant Galilean peasant some would have us believe, but supreme among men in the intellectual realm; and stated as the common-places of His knowledge, things which they have taken nineteen hundred centuries to spell out.

He affirmed the reality of the spiritual. He told men what they need is eternal life, and eternal life is not a quantity, but a quality, life that touches the infinite, that is homed in God, that takes in eternity. All this sighing after the spiritual is to be answered by preaching Jesus Christ as Lord, and bringing men into submission to Him. He will lead them into life, and they will find they have an answer to their deepest cry, the sense of the spiritual.

And then as to the passion for practical things. How is it manifested?

We are told we must have a social and ethical Gospel. Where will you find it?

It is a remarkable thing that these very men when they tell us what they want, refer to the Sermon on the Mount. Whose Gospel was that? It is the Gospel of our King. You say you want a practical Gospel, that this age must have a social and ethical Gospel. Well, here it is.

But Christianity as it delivers its message is more practical than the men who are crying for practical things. Men are saying, we want an ethical and social Gospel. We don't want to hear about the Cross. We have had enough of the Cross. Give us something social and practical. Christ is so practical that He never asks men to obey His laws unless they are regenerate.

Christ takes into account the paralysis in human life. You cannot build up a regenerated society unless you have regenerated men. You will find that Christianity is pre-eminently practical. It does not attempt to construct a living society out of dead matter, neither does it attempt to realize a pure order among corrupt men, neither does it attempt to give a perfect ethic to paralyzed individuals.

It takes hold of the man first, and remakes him, and then remakes society. It takes hold of the man fast bound in sin, and breaks his chains, and then tells him to walk upright. Men will never be influenced by a social Gospel until they have heard and obeyed the Gospel of regeneration.

Let us thank God for the wider outlook of the age in which we live.

Oh how many children are crying in the night, and with no language but a cry. Our business is to interpret the cry of the child to itself.

Men want something. They will sob out all sorts of foolish things, and tell us what they think they want. Never let us forget that they will never have the satisfactory answer to their profoundest and widest prayer save along the line of personal regeneration.

It is a sad thing indeed when a minister of Jesus Christ thinks of himself as an interesting entertainer, an intellectual instructor of his people merely, or a social reformer, or a political agent merely.

He ought to have something else to do. The principal work to which he is called wherever he may be sent, is that of bringing individuals into touch with spiritual realities, and in proportion as he is able to lead men to Christ individually, he is answering the cry of the age for the spiritual, for the practical; and contributing to that great visitation for which men are sighing and waiting in the darkness.

The voices of the age are full of hope. I know the other side. I know the pressure of the burden, and the apparent strength of sin. These are but the symptoms of a day. God is moving towards victory. May He make us fellow workers with Him.

Also by Parvus Magna Press

Foundations of Faith for New Believers – Leaders Manual

Foundations of Faith for new believers is a series of 10 Bible Studies around the basics of the Christian faith. The 10 subjects including Faith, Salvation and Prayer are easy to understand simple Bible studies that encourage the new Christian in their faith and encourage them to ask questions about their walk with God.

The Foundations of Faith series has sold over 30,000 copies since it was first published about 15 years ago and has helped thousands of new believers become valuable members of the congregation.

This is the Leaders Manual which has plenty of space for notes and comments for the study leader and you can also get a student's manual.

Paperback ISBN 978-1910372005

Kindle ISBN 978-1910372067

Foundations of Faith for New Believers – Students Manual

This is the Student Manual which is a great give-away, either at the start of the course or at the end as a prize for furthor study. All of the material contained in the leader's manual is here for the students.

Paperback ISBN 978-1910372012

The Evangelical Heritage Library

We have modernised the language of all these classic books, without losing the essential spirit and tone of the original work. We have also added many footnotes to explain cultural and social references that may not necessarily be known to the modern reader.

James Black – The Mystery of Preaching

In this incredible work James Black looks deeply into the art and science of preaching. He teaches the skills needed to construct deep and relevant sermons that excite and move the congregation and "prepare them for every good work".

This book is a must read for the new pastor as well as those older and well – experienced workmen – even if it's just as a reminder!

ISBN: 978-1-910372-07-4 Paperback
ISBN: 978-1-910372-08-1 Paperback
ISBN 978-1-910372-09-8 Kindle/Kobo

James Black – Around the Guns

James Black manages to communicate the gospel with a clarity and fervour that are infectious and although his illustrations and stories may seem at first to be dated and without application in this modern computerised world, the underlying message comes through loud and clear.

I enjoyed transcribing this book thoroughly and more than once found my prayer closet to deal with issues in my own heart that I felt I had already dealt with years ago.

I hope this volume blesses you and your ministry just as it has blessed mine.

ISBN 978-1-910372-10-4 Paperback
ISBN 978-1-910372-11-1 Paperback
ISBN 978-1-910372-12-8 eBook

S D Gordon – Quiet talks about Jesus

S D Gordon's classic work on the life and ministry of Jesus is a masterful compelling book that draws the reader alongside the author and leads them directly to the foot of the cross.

This incredible work has been a favourite with Christians for over 100 years!

As with all Evangelical Heritage Library books we have modernised the text and supplied copious footnotes and annotations to help the reader get the most out of this incredible book!

ISBN 978-1-910372-10-4 Paperback
ISBN 978-1-910372-11-1 Paperback
ISBN 978-1-910372-12-8 eBook

www.ingramcontent.com/pod-product-compliance
Lightning Source LLC
Chambersburg PA
CBHW061338040426
42444CB00011B/2978